CONTROVERSIES

| Food

# Other books in the Current Controversies series

# ▍Food

*Jan Grover, Book Editor*

**GREENHAVEN PRESS**

*An imprint of Thomson Gale, a part of The Thomson Corporation*

Detroit • New York • San Francisco • New Haven, Conn. • Waterville, Maine • London

Christine Nasso, *Publisher*
Elizabeth Des Chenes, *Managing Editor*

© 2008 The Gale Group.

Star logo is a trademark and Gale and Greenhaven Press are registered trademarks used herein under license.

*For more information, contact:*
Greenhaven Press
27500 Drake Rd.
Farmington Hills, MI 48331-3535
Or you can visit our Internet site at http://www.gale.com

Cover photograph reproduced by permission of © Jean-Bernard Vernier/Corbis Sygma.

LIBRARY OF CONGRESS CATALOGING-IN-PUBLICATION DATA

Food / Jan Grover, book editor.
    p. cm. -- (Current controversies)
  Includes bibliographical references and index.
  ISBN-13: 978-0-7377-3793-6 (hardcover)
  ISBN-13: 978-0-7377-3794-3 (pbk.)
  1. Diet--United States. 2. Nutrition policy--United States. I. Grover, Jan.
  TX360.U6F62 2008
  363.8'62--dc22
                                                              2007039167

ISBN-10: 0-7377-3793-X (hardcover)
ISBN-10: 0-7377-3794-8 (pbk.)

Printed in the United States of America
10 9 8 7 6 5 4 3 2 1

# Contents

## Chapter 1: What Controversies Surround Nutrition?

## Chapter 3: Are Fast and Snack Foods Responsible for Obesity Among Youth?

### Yes: Fast and Snack Foods Are Responsible for Current Levels of Obesity

America's food industry pushed snacking to children in the 1980s, then fast foods to their schools in the 1990s. The result has been an explosion of obesity among schoolchildren.

**No: Fast and Snack Foods Are Not Responsible for Current Levels of Obesity**

# Foreword

By definition, controversies are "discussions of questions in which opposing opinions clash" (Webster's Twentieth Century Dictionary Unabridged). Few would deny that controversies are a pervasive part of the human condition and exist on virtually every level of human enterprise. Controversies transpire between individuals and among groups, within nations and between nations. Controversies supply the grist necessary for progress by providing challenges and challengers to the status quo. They also create atmospheres where strife and warfare can flourish. A world without controversies would be a peaceful world; but it also would be, by and large, static and prosaic.

## The Series' Purpose

The purpose of the Current Controversies series is to explore many of the social, political, and economic controversies dominating the national and international scenes today. Titles selected for inclusion in the series are highly focused and specific. For example, from the larger category of criminal justice, Current Controversies deals with specific topics such as police brutality, gun control, white collar crime, and others. The debates in Current Controversies also are presented in a useful, timeless fashion. Articles and book excerpts included in each title are selected if they contribute valuable, long-range ideas to the overall debate. And wherever possible, current information is enhanced with historical documents and other relevant materials. Thus, while individual titles are current in focus, every effort is made to ensure that they will not become quickly outdated. Books in the Current Controversies series will remain important resources for librarians, teachers, and students for many years.

In addition to keeping the titles focused and specific, great care is taken in the editorial format of each book in the series. Book introductions and chapter prefaces are offered to provide background material for readers. Chapters are organized around several key questions that are answered with diverse opinions representing all points on the political spectrum. Materials in each chapter include opinions in which authors clearly disagree as well as alternative opinions in which authors may agree on a broader issue but disagree on the possible solutions. In this way, the content of each volume in Current Controversies mirrors the mosaic of opinions encountered in society. Readers will quickly realize that there are many viable answers to these complex issues. By questioning each author's conclusions, students and casual readers can begin to develop the critical thinking skills so important to evaluating opinionated material.

Current Controversies is also ideal for controlled research. Each anthology in the series is composed of primary sources taken from a wide gamut of informational categories including periodicals, newspapers, books, United States and foreign government documents, and the publications of private and public organizations. Readers will find factual support for reports, debates, and research papers covering all areas of important issues. In addition, an annotated table of contents, an index, a book and periodical bibliography, and a list of organizations to contact are included in each book to expedite further research.

Perhaps more than ever before in history, people are confronted with diverse and contradictory information. During the Persian Gulf War, for example, the public was not only treated to minute-to-minute coverage of the war, it was also inundated with critiques of the coverage and countless analyses of the factors motivating U.S. involvement. Being able to sort through the plethora of opinions accompanying today's major issues, and to draw one's own conclusions, can be a complicated and frustrating struggle. It is the editors' hope that Current Controversies will help readers with this struggle.

# Introduction

*"As fewer Americans grow foods or live in proximity to farms, the sense of seasonality and ripeness has diminished."*

From films such as *Supersize Me*, the 2004 documentary that followed Morgan Spurlock's thirty day fast-food binge, to articles and news stories detailing the latest scare of contaminated food, the American diet often takes center stage in the media and public debates. Because of the constant food dialogue, there has probably never been a more exciting time for people who enjoy food than now, which is directly related to the ubiquity of fast food, take-out food, and restaurant food.

As the average American diet has narrowed to a small range of foods—ground beef, deep-fried potatoes, soda pop—it has prompted a reaction. People who want a wider range of food have aggressively sought it out. Some found what they were looking for at local farmers' markets, which have expanded from an estimated 300 in 1972 to 4,385 in 2006. People who deplore the decline of diversified small farms have joined the community-supported agriculture (CSA) movement, in which farmers sell shares of their annual crops to individuals and families, some of whom also help with planting and harvesting. Food cooperatives, once limited almost entirely to the Upper Midwest, now number almost 5,000, offering members an impressive variety of staples that have long since disappeared from supermarket shelves (for example, big selections of dried legumes, dried fruits, specialty flours, and nuts). Artisanal cheesemakers can be found now in every part of the country, making both traditional and innovative sheep, goat, and cow cheeses on a small scale and selling them, for the most part, through farmers' markets and food cooperatives.

Two of the chief factors bringing these new food institutions most vividly into focus are the broader issues of global warming and global trade. Even people who are not particularly interested in finding the perfect locally grown peach are frequently distressed to learn that on average, a supermarket peach or head of lettuce travels 1,500 miles to reach them—about 25 percent farther than it did in 1980. This is because trade in produce and meat has become global. Fresh fruits and vegetables in most American grocery stores are as likely to come from Argentina, Chile, Peru, New Zealand, Australia, Israel, Mexico, and South Africa as from within the United States. Most frozen apple juice concentrate currently comes from China. As nutritionist Joan Dye Gussow once quipped about a head of iceberg lettuce, we're "burning lots at petroleum to ship cold water around."

As fewer Americans grow foods or live in proximity to farms, the sense of seasonality and ripeness has diminished. Shoppers expect to be able to buy strawberries and melons in December (when they come from Chile and New Zealand) and ripe apples and squashes in July (when they come from Argentina and South Africa). They are content with "fresh" foods that were green when they were harvested and that have traveled for ten days before reaching supermarket shelves. In part, this is because as agricultural land near America's cities has been developed for homes and office parks, people are no longer familiar with the taste of locally grown and perfectly ripened food. It is also because even with shipping costs, food grown in other countries is less expensive than food grown in the United States.

Increasingly, a sizeable subset of Americans has concluded that conventional foods contribute to global warming because they are being shipped from farther and farther away. Such shoppers are seeking out locally and regionally grown food, often organic, reasoning that its greater expense is more than offset by the support it provides to local farmers, the care with which it was raised, and the enjoyment its superior flavor provides.

To the extent that local and regional food production diminishes carbon emissions from global transport, it represents a good that anyone can applaud. But the global food trade has a positive side as well: When it affords farmers in developing countries opportunities to earn better livings through fair trade than they could locally, many Americans want to support them. So the issues of global warming and global trade in food are by no means simple and clear-cut. Like everything else involved in the world trade in food today, they are interconnected.

While a greater variety of food production and food choice has increased options for consumers, it has only added to the already robust debate surrounding food production. The authors of the viewpoints in *Current Controversies: Food* present a variety of opinions on such debates as nutrition guidelines, food safety, and the impact of fast and snack food on youth. From the fundamental questions of diet to more advanced discussions of food safety techniques, food is one debate that should interest and involve everyone.

# CHAPTER 1

# What Controversies Surround Nutrition?

# The Politics of Food

*Marian Burros*

*Marian Burros is a food columnist for the* New York Times, *where she has worked for twenty-one years. She has won an Emmy Award for consumer reporting.*

The headlines about food [in 2006] read like a remarkable replay of Woody Allen's *Sleeper*, in which the things Americans think they should eat more of—lettuce and spinach—were suddenly the ones that could make them sick, or even kill them.

Yet critics of American agribusiness [the system of large-scale agriculture and food production], like Marion Nestle, a professor in the Department of Nutrition, Food Studies and Public Health at New York University, and the author of *What to Eat*, (2006) see an upside to all the bad news.

"This is the year everyone discovered that food is about politics and people can do something about it," she said. "In a world in which people feel more and more distant from global forces that control their lives, they can do something by, as the British put it, 'voting with your trolley,' their word for shopping cart."

## Food Safety in a Broken System

Eric Schlosser, author of *Fast Food Nation* (2001), about the horrors of industrialized food for the animals, the workers and the consumer, is equally upbeat. "Those negative events brought attention to the problems," he said [of 2006]. "Even the growers think the system is broken and has to be fixed," he added, referring to the California spinach farmers, who are now demanding that the government step in and set some rules about growing and processing produce.

Food safety isn't the only place Mr. Schlosser sees progress. "There is growing bipartisan consensus on obesity," he said. Former President Bill Clinton "brokered a deal with soft drink and snack food companies to remove sodas and junk food from schools," he added, and "Governors Mike Huckabee of Arkansas and Arnold Schwarzenegger of California have made nutrition in schools an important priority."

---

*The organics movement went mainstream [in 2006]. . . as Wal-Mart rolled out a wide selection of food bearing the United States Department of Agriculture's organic certification.*

---

[Two thousand six] was the year when Americans got in touch with their food, and its varied political and social connections came into focus in different media. *The Nation* devoted an entire issue, developed in collaboration with Alice Waters of Chez Panisse restaurant in Berkeley, to food. Michael Pollan's *Omnivore's Dilemma* (2006), a book that took a look at industrial agriculture and other topics, became a best seller. *Fast Food Nation* was made into a film by the director Richard Linklater.

## Animal Welfare Becomes a Food Issue

Partly as a result of the renewed focus on where food comes from, animal welfare groups like People for the Ethical Treatment of Animals, once relegated to fringe status, have captured some attention. Animal rights supporters persuaded officials in Chicago to ban foie gras [foie gras are the enlarged livers of force-fed ducks and geese] because they say force-feeding ducks and geese is cruel.

Whole Foods threatened to terminate its contract with a California duck grower because he processed and distributed the products of a foie gras producer. The supermarket chain has stopped selling live lobsters, it says, until it can figure out how to keep them more comfortable on their trip from ocean to fish counter. Lobster "condos" have been suggested.

## The Organic Movement: Too Successful?

The organics movement went mainstream [in 2006], too, as Wal-Mart rolled out a wide selection of food bearing the United States Department of Agriculture's organic certification. The chain also vowed to price these products only slightly higher than conventional foods.

But there were signs that organics may have become too successful for their own good. Once welcomed as the savior of the small farmer and the conscientious eater, organic farming has lost some of its luster, dulled by large operators who follow the letter of the law but ignore the larger principles that once characterized the organic movement.

Today the word no longer stands for small-scale farming and animals raised in a traditional pastoral setting. As Mr. Pollan wrote in the *New York Times* in 2001, about the dairy farms operated by the organic milk producer Horizon, "thousands of cows that never encounter a blade of grass spend their days confined to a fenced dry lot, eating (certified organic) grain and tethered to milking machines three times a day."

The Department of Agriculture is now considering allowing salmon farmers to call their fish organic even if the fish are fed nonorganic fishmeal. The increasingly loose meaning of the word has led some consumers, who once bought anything labeled organic, to rely on new signifiers, like grass-fed, sustainable or local.

It is not only individual shoppers who are choosing to vote with their food dollars. Tired of waiting for the federal government to act, local governments have stepped in. New York City banned trans fats in restaurants and told restaurants with standardized recipes that they must provide easy access to calorie information. Other municipal and state governments are requiring public institutions to buy more nutritious, locally produced food.

## Scale in Food Production and Distribution Has Become Problematic

The slow drip-drip-drip of foodborne outbreaks over the last 20 years has not desensitized people to the fact that food can harbor harmful bacteria; it has made them skittish [a harmful strain of *E. coli* bacteria, commonly associated with undercooked ground beef and canned foods]. After the outbreak of *E. coli* 0157:H7 in spinach in August [2006], sales of the vegetable plummeted 60 percent. With several outbreaks [in 2006], including one involving *E. coli* at the Taco Bell chain, the idea that eating local may be safer is taking hold. When the fruits or vegetables from dozens of farms are combined before shipping, the opportunities for contamination are greatly increased. The discovery of contaminated produce is happening at a time when advice about eating more fruits and vegetables seems to be having an impact. So concerns about safety may be contributing to the success of local farmers' markets.

"I see this happening everywhere, and it is enormous," Ms. Nestle said. "It's the recognition that food ties into extremely important social, economic, environmental and institutional issues. Ordinary people don't have access to these really important issues except through food."

# Government Dietary Guidelines Are Political, Not Scientific

*Walter C. Willett*

*Walter C. Willett, MD, chairs the Department of Nutrition at the Harvard School of Public Health and is a professor of medicine at the Harvard Medical School.*

During the dark ages of dietary advice—from which we are just emerging—guidelines for good nutrition were based on guess-work and good intentions. I [want] to share with you what solid science is teaching us about the long-term effects of diet on health. The lessons are exciting. They show that a delicious, satisfying diet based on whole grains, healthy oils, fruits, vegetables, and good sources of protein can help you stay healthy and active to an old age.

Another reason for writing this was to challenge the misleading advice embodied in the U.S. Department of Agriculture's ubiquitous Food Guide Pyramid. When the department announced it was considering revising the thirteen-year-old pyramid, my colleagues and I were delighted. . . . But politics and business as usual ultimately trumped science, and the USDA's new MyPyramid offers even less guidance on healthy eating than its predecessor. . . .

## The Importance of Diet in Human Health

Over the past twenty-five years, my colleagues and I have been continually surprised by the impact of diet on the risks of a host of chronic diseases. That dietary decisions could significantly affect the chances of heart disease, various cancers,

Walter C. Willett, "Preface" and "Building a Better Pyramid," *Eat, Drink, and Be Healthy*. New York: Free Press, 2005, pp. 7–16. Copyright © 2001 by President and Fellows of Harvard College. Reprinted with the permission of Simon & Schuster Adult Publishing Group.

cataracts, and even serious birth defects was not appreciated by the nutrition community until relatively recently. And many aspects of diet that were off the nutrition science radar screen, such as trans fat intake, glycemic load [a ranking system for the impact of carbohydrates in food] and low intakes of folic acid and vitamin D, have emerged as important factors in long-term health. You may not be aware of these topics, or perhaps have heard about them only in passing, even though a better understanding can be crucial to attaining long-term health. This [article] will guide you to make better dietary decisions for yourself and your family.

---

*When it comes to diet, knowing what's good and what's bad isn't easy.*

---

My current effort to understand the long-term effects of diet on health began in the late 1970s when I realized that people were being given strong advice about what to eat and what to avoid, but that direct evidence to support these recommendations was often weak or nonexistent. A key missing element was data based on detailed dietary intakes from many individuals that could be related to their future development of heart disease, various cancers, and other health problems. Of course, information on medical history, smoking, physical activity, and other lifestyle variables would be needed to isolate the effects of diet. Fortunately, at this time I was already investigating the relation of cigarette smoking to heart disease within the Nurses' Health Study, an ongoing study of over 121,000 women across the United States, and this appeared to be an ideal group in which to investigate the long-term consequences of various diets. The first step was to develop a standardized method of dietary assessment for such a large population; many colleagues were skeptical that this was possible, perhaps appropriately so. Borrowing on work done at Harvard in the 1940s, we developed a series of self-administered dietary questionnaires and were able to document their validity in a series of detailed evaluations. Since 1980 we have been following women in this study with periodic updating of dietary and other information and have also added large cohorts of men and additional women. Although our large prospective studies have provided a unique and powerful flow of information about diet and health, the best understanding of a topic as complex as diet and health should incorporate evidence from all available sources. . . .

## Dietary Advice Is Confusing

When it comes to diet, knowing what's good and what's bad isn't easy. The food industry spends billions of dollars a year to influence your choices. Diet gurus promote the latest fads, while the media serves up near daily helpings of often flip-flopping nutrition news. Supermarkets and fast-food restaurants offer advice, as do cereal boxes and a sea of Internet sites.

Where can you turn as a source of reliable information on healthy eating? The U.S. Department of Agriculture (USDA) touts its new food pyramid and "food guidance system" as aids to help you make healthier food choices. In reality, these tools help farmers and food companies more than they will help you.

---

*At best, MyPyramid stands as a missed opportunity to improve the health of millions of people.*

---

## Turning to the USDA Pyramid Is a Mistake

Through the Food Guide Pyramid, now called MyPyramid, the USDA presents what it wants you to think of as rock-solid nutrition information that rises above the jungle of misinformation and contradictory claims. What it really offers is wishy-washy, scientifically unfounded advice on an absolutely vital topic—what to eat.

The original Food Guide Pyramid, unveiled in 1992, was built on shaky scientific ground. It included six food groups, each labeled with recommended daily servings. At the foundation sat an admonition to load up on highly refined starches, while the top was crowned with a "Use Sparingly" group that included fats, oils, and sweets. In between were fruits, vegetables, protein, and dairy.

Over the next thirteen years, research from around the globe eroded the Food Guide Pyramid at all levels. Results from scores of large and small studies chipped away at its foundation (carbohydrates), middle (meat and milk), and tip (fats). The USDA never renovated the Pyramid, but left it to crumble under the weight of new scientific evidence.

---

*When it (finally) came time to "fix" the [Food] Pyramid, lobbying and politics took center stage, while science and . . . health . . . took a back seat.*

---

Taking a cue from television reality shows, the agriculture department gave the Pyramid an extreme makeover in April 2005. It tipped the Pyramid on its side and painted it with a rainbow of brightly colored bands running vertically from the tip to the base. A jaunty stick figure runs up stairs chiseled into the left side. That's it—no labels, no text, not even the equivalent of a nutritional Rosetta stone to help you decipher what it means. For that you need a computer and a connection to the Internet.

The good news about the makeover is that the USDA finally took a wrecking ball to its dangerously outmoded Pyramid. The bad news is that its replacement doesn't offer any real information to help you make healthy choices, and continues to recommend foods that aren't essential to good health and that may even be detrimental in the quantities included in MyPyramid.

At best, MyPyramid stands as a missed opportunity to improve the health of millions of people. At worst, the lack of information and downright misinformation it conveys contribute to overweight, poor health, and unnecessary early deaths. . . .

## How the USDA Pyramid Got Its Shape

The thing to keep in mind about the Pyramid is that it comes from the arm of the federal government responsible for promoting American agriculture. It doesn't come from agencies established to monitor and protect our health, like the Institute of Medicine or the National Institutes of Health. And there's the root of the problem—what's good for agricultural interests isn't necessarily good for the people who eat their products.

Serving two masters is tricky business, especially when one of them includes persuasive, connected, and well-funded representatives of the formidable meat, dairy, and sugar industries. The end result of the tug-of-war between the food industry and nutrition science is a set of positive, feel-good, all-inclusive recommendations that distort what could be the single most important tool for improving your health and the health of the nation—guidelines on healthful eating.

## Food Politics

When it (finally) came time to "fix" the Pyramid, lobbying and politics took center stage, while science and the health of the American people took a back seat.

The story begins with the Dietary Guidelines for Americans, a document the USDA says provides "authoritative advice for people two years and older about how good dietary habits can promote health and reduce risk for major chronic diseases." By law, these guidelines must be revised every five years. It is supposed to be a scholarly and scientific process, but is often a free-for-all among lobbyists for agribusinesses [the system of large-scale agriculture and food production], food companies, and special-interest groups.

In 2003, a new executive director was appointed for the center. Curiously, the person chosen for the job was an expert in animal nutrition whose previous jobs had been with the National Livestock and Meat Board, the National Pork Producers Association, and the National Pork Board.

The 2005 revision began as in past years—the USDA selected a committee of thirteen respected nutrition experts from across the country. The committee sifted through the latest research and time-tested knowledge to figure out what we know about the American diet and healthful eating.

But a funny thing happened on the way to the final report. Instead of writing the Dietary Guidelines for Americans 2005, the committee was told to hand over its findings to a second committee charged with translating the science into useful guidelines. That committee was never formed. How the Department of Agriculture developed the final guidelines isn't clear, since the process was so obscure.

This handoff created subtle but important shifts in emphasis in the final guidelines. For example, the committee said that less than 1 percent of our daily calories should come from harmful trans fats, which are found in many prepared foods. What the Dietary Guidelines for Americans ultimately said is that we should keep trans fat intake "as low as possible," a recommendation that is open to interpretation. The committee specified that whole grains should account for *at least* half of daily carbohydrate intake. MyPyramid gives this a gentle but telling twist, "Make half your grains whole," which implies that half should be refined. . . .

## Why Guidelines Matter

If the Dietary Guidelines and MyPyramid were merely optional recommendations and diet aids, we might be able to overlook the hijacking of the process used to create them. But the Dietary Guidelines set the standards for all federal nutrition programs. These include food stamps, school lunch programs, and food services for those serving in the armed forces as well as in federal prisons. The Dietary Guidelines and Pyramid also help determine what foods and food products Americans buy. In other words, they influence how billions of dollars are spent each year. No wonder food companies lobby so hard for changes that will benefit them, not the American public.

Some recommendations on diet and nutrition are misguided because they are based on inadequate or incomplete information. That hasn't been the case for the USDA's pyramids. They are wrong because they brush aside evidence on healthful eating that has been carefully assembled over the past forty years.

# Health Studies Overemphasize the Impact of Diet

*Barry Glassner*

*Barry Glassner is a professor of sociology at the University of Southern California and the author of* The Culture of Fear.

Optimally, the effects of diet would be assessed the same way drugs are tested, through experiments in which some people are given the substance in question while others take sugar pills, and neither group knows which it has received. Obviously, that sort of study is close to impossible when it comes to diet. You can't give one person a T-bone and another tofu and have them believe they are eating the same thing. The closest that nutrition researchers come to randomized trials are experiments in which they assign people to eat particular foods rather than give them free choice. That scheme reduces the likelihood that other commonalities among people are responsible for differences in their rates of disease. But as Gina Kolata and others have pointed out, such experiments are difficult to pull off successfully because people have a hard time sticking to mandated diets.

---

*Optimally, the effects of diet would be assessed the same way drugs are tested, through experiments.*

---

The consequences of errors are potentially greater in studies of diet than in other sorts of research on how our behaviors affect our health. If, because of faulty information, a study concludes that smoking increases the risk of lung cancer by only 2,000 percent rather than 3,000 percent (the amount other studies have shown), the moral of the story remains the same. Either way, there can be little doubt that smokers run a significantly greater risk than nonsmokers. By contrast, studies of the effects of foods on heart disease and cancer often show an increased risk of only 20 or 30 percent. A few errors in measurement and the danger disappears almost entirely.

In many of the studies, the number of people in the group that ate the purportedly unhealthy food and got sick is shockingly small. A report from the Nurses Health Study that appeared in the *New England Journal of Medicine* and led to a number of frightening news reports is a case in point. Women who eat beef, pork, or lamb every day have two and a half times greater risk of developing colon cancer over a six-year period compared with women who eat red meat less than once a month, Willett and his colleagues reported.

---

*In many studies, the number of people in the group that ate the purportedly unhealthy food and got sick is shockingly small.*

---

With findings like that, it is easy to appreciate why Willett responded so concisely to a question from a reporter. Asked how much meat people should eat, he gave a one-word reply: "Zero." But when I examined the journal article, I discovered that the "two and a half times" figure was based on a small number of women. A total of 150 of the 89,000 women in the study developed colon cancer over a six-year period. Of those who said they ate red meat less than once a month, 14 developed colon cancer, compared with 16 who said they ate red meat every day. If just a few women inadvertently misinformed the researchers about how much meat they ate or their health status, the front-page headlines about the risk of meat eating may well have been off base. . . .

To hear advocates of the doctrine of naught tell it, the scientific evidence is clear and decisive, and no scientist in his right mind seriously doubts the major tenets of the reigning view. In reality, however, as historian Felipe Fernandez-Armesto of Oxford University has written, "one of the few verifiable laws about dietetics is that the experts always disagree."

---

*A diet that is harmful to one person may be consumed with impunity by another.*

---

In the course of my research, I discovered many well-versed scientists who challenge the conventional wisdom. Some, such as James Le Fanu of England and Uffe Ravnskov of Sweden, are physicians without academic positions, who take it upon themselves to study the scientific research and publish books with titles like *The Rise and Fall of Modern Medicine* and *The Cholesterol Myths*. Others are prominent researchers like Powles at Cambridge, whose findings turn the doctrine of naught on its head. He has identified groups of Greeks, Italians, and Japanese whose death rates from heart disease dropped as their meat consumption and blood cholesterol levels increased.

Closer to home, I came upon articles by Marcia Angell, former editor of the *New England Journal of Medicine* and a senior lecturer in the Department of Social Medicine at Harvard Medical School. "Although we would all like to believe that changes in diet or lifestyle can greatly improve our health," Angell wrote in an essay in 1994, "the likelihood is that, with a few exceptions such as smoking cessation, many if not most such changes will produce only small effects. And the effects may not be consistent. A diet that is harmful to one person may be consumed with impunity by another."

In an interview, Angell told me that the incessant warnings about foods may even do harm. "There is an analogy," she said, "to the story of the boy who cried wolf. If you're always ascribing things to diet and lifestyle, then when you do hear about something that's based on good evidence and really does have an effect, you've gotten cynical about it. You have just heard too much, often contradictory stuff, to take real threats seriously. A good example is cigarettes. They are a real threat, and yet, a lot of people look at smoking cigarettes as no worse than eating hot dogs."

I asked Angell why seemingly well-meaning epidemiogists and nutrition researchers would make the dangers of foods seem greater than they are. "They want grants and publicity," Angell replied. "Medical research is no longer done in an ivory tower. The National Institutes of Health and various companies that fund the research read the newspaper too. Publicity is very good for researchers."

Besides, she let me know, scientists who study the connection between food and disease may be believers themselves. "Researchers, even though they're supposed to be totally impartial, often carry with them sets of biases, and if they want to show something, they often work very hard to show that. They conclude what they want to conclude when there are other possible conclusions that would flow equally from their data."

---

*[Medical researchers] conclude what they want to conclude when there are other possible conclusions that would flow equally from their data.*

---

Where, I asked Angell, does that leave the public? Are there foods that people really should shun?

"Within limits they should eat the way they want to eat," Angell replies. "What are the limits? I think they should eat in moderation, and I think they should eat as varied a diet as possible because that's good insurance. You don't put all of your eggs in one basket, or in this case, your health in one egg. You try to cover the waterfront because you're operating from a position of extraordinary ignorance, so your best bet is to eat a varied diet."

*Eat what you want.* I heard that advice not only from Marcia Angell, but from my personal physician as well. In fact, he had me conduct a little experiment that further strengthened his point.

His advice to eat what I want came initially during an annual physical exam, after he informed me that my cholesterol numbers had gone up compared with the previous year. I asked if I should change my diet, and in response, he took out a pad and scribbled a prescription for a cholesterol-lowering drug while instructing me—in a wearied voice, as if to a medical student who had asked a dumb question—that changing my diet probably will not help my heart or any other organ and I should eat what I want to eat.

---

*If some people are healthier for having eschewed some foods, the reason may well be psychological.*

---

Mild humiliation is a price I pay for having my medical examinations performed by Ricardo Hahn, of the Department of Family Medicine at the University of Southern California, where I work. All things being equal, I would not voluntarily put myself in the position of being corrected by a fellow professor while I sit naked except for my shorts and socks. But when it comes to medical care, things are never equal, and I prefer Hahn over docs who take at face value what they read in the health section of the local newspaper.

"What we think we know about nutrition is not supported by real scientific inquiry," he told me on a subsequent occasion. Little biological evidence exists, he said, to support the claims of those who caution against particular foods. If some people are healthier for having eschewed those foods, the reason may well be psychological. "Because of the placebo effect, people feel better when they adopt certain dietary habits," Hahn contended.

When I reminded him that his views are at odds with what one hears from physicians at the American Heart Association [AHA] and diet advisory panels of the U.S. government, he recommended I do a small study myself to see how much those docs are really willing to attribute to diet.

"You have to ask the right question," said Hahn. Ask general questions about whether diet matters, he advised, and you'll get platitudes in return. Force them instead to give a number—ask the percentage that diet contributes to particular diseases—and they'll sing a different tune.

Hahn encouraged me to test his hypothesis on the then-president of the American Heart Association, David Faxon, a cardiologist at the University of Chicago with whom Hahn had worked in the past. I should call Faxon and insist he be precise, Hahn instructed.

And sure enough, when I reached Faxon and asked him the percentage that diet contributes to heart disease, the question seemed to stop him in his tracks. "Wow. That's a very difficult question to answer, frankly," he said. "I guess part of the reason it's hard to answer is, you don't have as much information about the importance of diet on cardiovascular risk. We have a lot more information on some of the things that are affected by diet and, the effects of drugs on those things, for instance, cholesterol."

Faxon went on to say that as a clinician he believes that diet matters more for some people than for others, and he made general statements endorsing the Mediterranean Diet Pyramid and the care with which AHA committees come up with their dietary guidelines. Then he acknowledged the relative lack of knowledge about the effect of diet on heart disease. "We have limited information in a number of studies on dietary modifications to cardiovascular risks," he said. "But when you compare it with the wealth of information that we have on other things, the data is really small."

Faxon in turn urged me to talk with Ronald Krauss, the principal author of the AHA's dietary guidelines. An M.D. and senior staff scientist in the Life Sciences Division at the Lawrence National Laboratory in Berkeley, California, Krauss has also served on the Food and Nutrition Board of the National Academy of Sciences.

I reached Krauss by phone and asked him to estimate the percentage that diet contributes to disease, and he answered my question with a question. "Are you talking about all of diet and all of disease?"

I suggested we focus on his specialty, heart disease.

"I suppose to say the word 'important' is not enough," he tried, and I respectfully asked if he could be more specific.

"I don't even know where to start in trying to answer that question," Krauss said, audibly annoyed. After a little more prodding, he said that, on average, heart disease is attributable half to genetic factors and half to lifestyle factors such as diet, exercise, smoking, and body weight.

---

*On average, heart disease is attributable half to genetic factors and half to lifestyle factors such as diet, exercise, smoking, and body weight.*

---

From having looked at some of Krauss's published papers, I know that much of his own research explores how genetic factors influence people's responses to diet. He and other researchers have documented that individuals react very differently to low-fat or reduced-salt diets, for example, depending upon their genetic predispositions. One person's LDI or blood pressure plunges, while someone else's remains nearly unchanged.

Someday doctors might be able to estimate how much difference a particular change in diet would make for a particular person, on the basis of one's genetic profile and other information.

Suddenly, I felt incredibly well protected against heart disease.

# Obesity Is Not a Public Health Issue

*Radley Balko*

*Radley Balko previously worked as a policy analyst for the libertarian Cato Institute, specializing in vice and civil liberties issues. He is a columnist for* FoxNews.com, *a senior editor for* Reason *magazine, and has been widely published. He keeps a libertarian blog (TheAgitator.com) and lives outside of Washington, D.C.*

Obesity Policy Report [a food industry advocacy organization] has become a leading insider newsletter for lawmakers, regulators, food industry executives, and nutrition advocates. The following is a Q&A the publication ran in 2005 with frequent TCS [Tech Central Station] contributor and Cato Institute [a libertarian think tank] policy analyst Radley Balko.

**OPR:** *You're completing a white paper for Cato on obesity that will be published later this year. What's your thesis?*

**Radley Balko:** It's an overview of the obesity debate, with an emphasis on personal responsibility and consumer choice. It will first make the case that obesity is fundamentally a private issue, not a legitimate "public health" issue within the purview of government. Second, it will examine whether the obesity problem is really as dire as it's made out to be by activists and the media. Third, it will look at many anti-obesity initiatives and examine their flaws and features. Finally, it will make the case that the free market has done a more than adequate job addressing these problems, and I'll make recommendations for how the government can help fight obesity by restricting its influence in the food marketplace.

Radley Balko, "Private Matters and 'Public Health,'" *TCS Daily, TechCentralStation .com*, February 7, 2005. Reproduced by permission.

*From a libertarian standpoint, what's at stake in the war over obesity, and the way in which government and special interest groups are trying to solve the problem?*

Quite a bit, I think. The danger here comes with the one-two punch of an increasingly socialized healthcare system and an ever-expanding nanny state. More and more, we as individuals are being held financially responsible for the health and well-being of everyone else—your high cholesterol shows up on my tax bill or in my insurance premiums. When that happens, it becomes much easier for government to justify further intrusion into our choices as diners and consumers, on the premise that "we're saving taxpayers money." That's pretty scary. We need to reverse both trends. We need to make healthcare more private and market-oriented. But we also need to let people make their own decisions about what they eat, and make clear that they and they alone will bear the consequences of those decisions.

## The Nanny Culture and Obesity

*You specialize in analyzing the "nanny culture." With obesity, who are the biggest offenders, in your view—the biggest nannies? Government is often accused of being a nanny, but in the case of obesity, many special interest groups criticize it for not doing nearly enough.*

I find that troubling—that there are those who think government hasn't done enough. Many of the same groups pushing for more government action on obesity are also active on the anti-alcohol (Center for Science in the Public Interest comes to mind) and anti-tobacco (the Robert Wood Johnson Foundation comes to mind) fronts. There, we've seen them push some pretty severe restrictions on consumer choice, civil liberties, and due process. Given that they're using many of the same arguments in the obesity debate that they've used in the tobacco and alcohol debates, it's frightening to think what types of policies they might push down the road.

Where government has intervened in matters as private and intimate as what we put into our bodies, we've seen some pretty drastic and unintended consequences. The forbidden fruit effect has led to a scourge of underage binge drinking. Jurisdictions with high cigarette taxes have spawned black markets that fund crime syndicates and international terrorism organizations. And we've all seen the devastating effects wrought by the failed war on drugs.

*For some reason, our society has put a premium on longevity. Anything that shaves minutes off of our lives is by definition considered something that ought to be taxed or restricted.*

## A Government Role in the Obesity Wars?

*In your opinion, what's the worst thing the government could do to "fight" obesity?*

The worst thing it can do is treat obesity as a "public health" problem or, for that matter, "fight" obesity at all. Government is too prone to the influence of special interest groups and congressmen out to promote the industries and agriculture of their home districts for us to trust it to dictate or influence something as important as our diet and our health. Look at the disaster that is the Food Pyramid. Look at the [Centers for Disease Control and Prevention] CDC's infamous, bogus, "400,000 annual deaths attributable to obesity" statistic. Look at the ridiculous BMI [body mass index] system, where some of the world's greatest athletes are lumped in with "obesity" figures.

We shouldn't be restricting liberty even if science proves the most alarmist claims about obesity correct. But the science is all over the place. There's lots of research coming out right now suggesting that all of this influence on weight may be killing people. It makes overweight people turn to dieting—

41

which almost always fails—instead of focusing on becoming more active, which doesn't do much for weight, but is far more beneficial for overall health than dieting.

The best way to ensure bad public policy is to pass reactionary laws at the height of a media frenzy. The president of the Robert Wood Johnson Foundation said at a conference [in June 2004] that "we need to act ahead of the science." I think that's the single worst thing we can do. We should wait for the science to become conclusive, so we can be sure what we are doing isn't unnecessary or, worse, counterproductive.

*What's the best thing government could do?*

Get out of the way. The free market consists of hundreds of millions of people engaging in voluntary, mutually beneficial transactions every day. It's the best way to allocate resources. It's arrogant to think that a handful of government bureaucrats or nutrition activists know more about what foods should be available to us than the collected wisdom of millions of self-interested people. If food some consider "bad" is available on the market, it's because there are people out there who enjoy it. It's offensive and condescending to say the average Joe is too dumb to know that a Hardee's Monster Thickburger slathered in cheese, bacon and mayonnaise, or a decadent, chocolaty dessert probably isn't all that good for him. He knows it's not the best thing for him. He chooses to accept the risk because he enjoys the indulgence. A free society doesn't use laws, taxes, or restrictions to deny him that indulgence.

For some reason, our society has put a premium on longevity. Anything that shaves minutes off of our lives is by definition considered something that ought to be taxed or restricted. But there are plenty of people out there who have probably heard that a cigarette or a slice of cake might take a few minutes off the ends of their lives, and they're willing to sacrifice those few minutes because, believe it or not, they want a cigarette or a slice of cake. Why is that decision any business of the government's? . . .

## Personal Responsibility and Corporate Responsibility

*Some argue that "personal responsibility" is just another way of the food industry saying, "Leave us alone so we can make lots of money." From a libertarian viewpoint, does the industry have a responsibility to its customers to provide them with healthier food?*

No. The only responsibility any industry or corporation has is to be honest and forthright about what it's putting on the market. If a company is making false claims about what it's selling, it should certainly be held accountable, and we have laws against fraud and false advertising for that.

But it's silly to expect the food industry to market products the public doesn't want. I'm baffled by the criticism of the fast food industry in particular, which has never really claimed to be in the health food business. Should Baskin-Robbins be held liable for not putting fresh fruits and vegetables on its menu, too? If not, why should McDonald's?

If consumers truly want healthier options, they'll indicate that preference by buying healthy. Until only recently, they hadn't been doing that. Now that they are, we've seen an explosion of grocery and restaurant options for carb-, calorie-, and fat-counters. That's the market in action. When corporations make money, they don't do so at the expense of consumers, they do so with the blessing of consumers. It takes two parties to make a sale. To the extent that there may be a problem here, it isn't with corporations, it's with consumer preference. If the nutrition activists want to launch privately-funded public relations campaigns aimed at changing consumer habits, I say bully to them.

But don't blame corporations for giving the public what it wants. That's what a market economy is all about.

# Bans of Certain Foods Are Absurd

### The Center for Consumer Freedom

*The Center for Consumer Freedom is a nonprofit coalition of restaurants, food companies, and consumers promoting personal responsibility and protection of the right of adults and parents to choose what they eat, drink, and how they enjoy themselves.*

Over the years, the growing cabal of diet dictators have proposed a litany of crazy proposals to tax, legislate, and litigate away many food and beverage choices. What follows are ten of their dumbest ideas:

*"We're going to sue them and sue them and sue them."*

As a grim precursor to a campaign of extermination-through-litigation, the Public Health Advocacy Institute (PHAI) recently convened its second annual meeting dedicated to suing American food producers into oblivion. Following their first conference, "intended to encourage and support litigation against the food industry," then-PHAI executive director Ben Kelley sent a letter to eight major food companies and restaurants insisting that they take responsibility for slimming America down. If food companies didn't force everyone to go on a diet, the letter warned, trial lawyers would sue.

*. . . and Sue Their Parents and Sue Their Doctors. . .*

If litigation against restaurants and food companies weren't enough, self-described movement leader John "Sue the Bastards" Banzhaf [an attorney who has sued food companies for PHAI] has a few other wacky notions. In true ambulance-chasing fashion, Banzhaf advocates suing doctors who don't adequately warn patients about obesity. He also urges lawsuits

"Ten Dumbest Food Cop Ideas" [Editorial], *Center for Consumer Freedom*, September 27, 2004, www.consumerfreedom.com/news_detail.cfm?headline=2651. Reproduced by permission.

against parents of obese children, saying lawyers should "go after parents with TVs in their [kids'] rooms."

## Banning Diet Soda in Schools

In an attempt to address childhood obesity, politicians in Texas, New York, Philadelphia, California and elsewhere have removed soft drinks from schools. But in their frenzy to control our kids' diets, they have also banned diet soda—a zero-calorie drink, last time we checked—along with everything else. Of course, the schools are still allowed to sell fruit juice, which often contains more calories than regular soda.

All of this comes without a shred of credible evidence linking soda—let alone diet soda—to childhood obesity. In fact, a recent study by six Harvard researchers found just the opposite.

---

*In its never-ending attempt to demonize a long list of foods, the CSPI has taken to labeling some items "food porn."*

---

## The "Zoning" Diet—Keep Restaurants Out of Town

"There is no reason we can't, through zoning and planning, regulate the location, density, or hours of junk-food outlets," write reliable food cops Tom Farley and Deborah Cohen [authors of *Prescription for a Healthy Nation*]. They're hardly alone in demanding draconian zoning restrictions on restaurants and food stores. Yale University's Kelly "Big Brother" Brownell also supports the idea. And after a Dunkin' Donuts opened up in Scituate, Massachusetts, PBS's [Public Broadcasting System, the public television network] Mark Fenton (a self-anointed "pedestrian advocate") took action. A member of the town's planning board, Fenton proposed a measure to prevent any new fast food restaurant from coming to town. Although the vote was 140–90 in favor, it narrowly failed to meet the two-thirds majority necessary to become law.

## Hiding Candy Behind the Counter

In its never-ending attempt to demonize a long list of foods, the Center for Science in the Public Interest (CSPI) has taken to labeling some items "food porn." But Public Health Institute lawyer Edward Bolen has taken CSPI's moniker even further. He is convinced that candy bars, chewing gum, and Tic-Tacs should be treated the same way as *Playboy* and *Penthouse*. Bolen advocates "putting nutritionally deficient foods behind the counter like you do with spray paint." Of course, his proposal risks creating what CSPI nutritionist Bonnie Leibman calls the problem of "forbidden fruit." By day, Leibman labors to put severe restrictions on our food choices. But by night she lets her own kids occasionally snack on treats to prevent them from developing an insatiable urge to indulge behind her back.

## No Sharing of Snacks at School

"Until further notice birthday or any other classroom treats will need to be purely nutritional and as free of sugar as possible. . . . Please do not be disturbed or disappointed when your sweet treats are denied by the teacher due to this new policy from the Department of Agriculture." That's from a letter sent home to the parents of students at Walnut Creek Elementary in Azle, Texas.

The letter came in response to an edict from Texas Agricultural Commissioner Susan Combs, who calls herself the "Food Czarina." She unilaterally prohibited hundreds of foods in Texas schools, and her dictates even prevent students from sharing treats with their friends. "Stop," Combs barks in true food cop fashion. "Step away from the junk food."

# National Food Czar

As crazy as Combs might sound, she's got company. In 1998, a panel of diet scolds organized by the National Academy of Sciences recommended a litany of new food regulations, including a mandate for a national "food czar" to centralize nutrition policies. A similar food czar has already been appointed in Scotland.

Hopefully, this lord and master of food doesn't take the job too literally, returning our diets to CSPI Executive Director Michael Jacobson's dream of eating like 18th-century serfs—feasting "on perhaps a pound of bread, a spud, and a couple of carrots per day."

*In the skewed world of these zealots, a childhood trip down the drugstore candy aisle is now as perilous as an under-age evening of barhopping.*

# Sin Tax on Restaurant Meals Under Four Dollars

Fast food restaurants in Canada were almost forced to ask "Would you like a fat tax with that?" after the Liberal Party in Ontario proposed an eight percent tax on meals under four dollars. The plan didn't go through, but only after food banks complained that the tax would "affect welfare kids and single moms, low-income seniors, and the working poor." Despite its failure in Canada, extra taxes on high-calorie snacks and other tasty foods could become a reality some day soon. Already, several state legislators in America have proposed these taxes on eating what you want.

# Carding for Candy

Anti-consumer gadflies trying to force an all-tofu diet on society are also taking cues from New Zealand, where the Ministry of Health recently proposed a new law extending the minimum purchase age requirements on liquor and cigarettes to such popular foods as soda, hamburgers, pie, candy, and chocolate. Ever on the lookout for oppressive new ideas, the American-based Public Health Institute has latched onto the Kiwis' [New Zealanders are affectionately nicknamed "Kiwis"] proposal. Ed Bolen, an attorney for the group, advocates similar alcohol- and tobacco-style age restrictions on the sale of popular foods throughout the U.S. In the skewed world of these zealots, a childhood trip down the drugstore candy aisle is now as perilous as an under-age evening of barhopping. Let's hope your kids have a designated tricycler.

## Completely Dismissing Personal Responsibility

Perhaps the worst idea of all is this one from CSPI's Margo Wootan: "We've got to move beyond personal responsibility." Wootan is hardly alone. Anti-soda crusader Harold Goldstein insists, "The delusion is that we all make free choices." And when the World Health Organization added a line referencing the "exercise of individual responsibility" to its anti-obesity strategy, CSPI raged: "Obesity is not merely a matter of individual responsibility. Such suggestions are naive and simplistic." Speaking of simplistic, lawsuit cheerleader John Banzhaf sums up the notion of personal responsibility as "crap."

# The Best Diet Is the Product of Common Sense

*Jacob Sullum*

*Jacob Sullum is a senior editor at the libertarian* Reason *magazine. He is the author of* Saying Yes: In Defense of Drug Use *(Tarcher/Penguin) and* For Your Own Good: The Anti-Smoking Crusade and the Tyranny of Public Health *(Free Press).*

What are we to make of Arthur Hoyte, a retired physician from Rockville, Maryland, who is suing KFC [Kentucky Fried Chicken] because he thought fried chicken was a health food? In a lawsuit sponsored by the Center for Science in the Public Interest [CSPI], Hoyte claims he had no idea the restaurant chain fries its food in partially hydrogenated vegetable oil. "If I had known that KFC uses an unnatural frying oil, and that the food was so high in trans fat, I would have reconsidered my choices," he says.

Aren't doctors supposed to be smart, at least when it comes to health-related issues? If Hoyte has no way of knowing about all the trans fat in KFC's dishes, what chance do the rest of us have?

## Protecting Us Against Our Own Food Choices

CSPI's would-be class action, based on Washington, D.C. consumer protection law, accuses the chain of failing to disclose "material facts" about its food and demands that it either stop using partially hydrogenated oil or post trans fat warning signs. According to CSPI Executive Director Michael Jacobson (who is not known for his rhetorical subtlety), KFC "recklessly

Jacob Sullum, "The Fried Logic of Food Police: Trans Fat in Fast Food? Who Knew?" *Reason Online*, August 18, 2006. Copyright 2006 by Reason Foundation, 3415 S. Sepulveda Blvd., Suite 400, Los Angeles, CA 90034, www.reason.com. Reproduced by permission.

puts its customers at risk of a Kentucky Fried Coronary" and is "making its unsuspecting consumers' arteries Extra Crispy." To support these claims, CSPI's online statement links to three pages of nutritional information about the KFC menu.

But who is that bearded, white-haired gentleman in the upper left corner of each page in this damning indictment? It turns out the trans fat secrets Colonel Sanders is keeping from his customers—information so arcane even a medical specialist cannot reasonably be expected to know it—[are] contained in a "Nutrition Guide" on KFC's Web site and on big, conspicuous posters in KFC outlets.

---

*The real goal is to impose CSPI's ideas about a proper diet on consumers who have different values and priorities.*

---

The use of partially hydrogenated vegetable oil by restaurants is widely known; they switched to it after groups like CSPI complained about the animal fat and tropical oils they had been using. At the time, the new fat was thought to be healthier, but subsequent research has indicated it may in fact be worse. A man of medicine like Dr. Hoyte surely was aware of this development.

The problem, from CSPI's point of view, is not that people don't know about trans fat in KFC's food but that they don't care. If there were a big enough demand for trans-fat-free fried chicken, KFC would make the switch to nonhydrogenated vegetable oil (which costs more and has a shorter shelf life). But it's possible that people who eat a lot of fried chicken don't worry about the nutritional profile of their food.

## Food Litigation Gone Mad

As usual, CSPI does not like the choices consumers are making and wants businesses to follow its preferences instead. The organization brags about using the threat of a lawsuit to pressure the leading soda manufacturers into an agreement aimed at removing sugar-sweetened beverages from public schools—a deal that is not likely to have a noticeable impact on students' waistlines but may inspire restrictions on adults, such as "junk-food-free" zones near schools. In Massachusetts, CSPI is threatening to sue Kellogg, maker of sugary breakfast cereals, and Viacom, owner of TV channels and cartoon characters used to market "nutritionally poor" food. CSPI argues that children are injured every time they see an ad for Apple Jacks or a box of SpongeBob SquarePants Pop-Tarts, whether or not their parents actually buy the product.

Each of these cases supposedly is about damage suffered and compensation owed. But the real goal is to impose CSPI's ideas about a proper diet on consumers who have different values and priorities. If this is in "the public interest," it's an interest the public itself is too benighted to recognize.

# Misleading Nutritional Advice Has Led to an Unsustainable Diet

*Michael Pollan*

*Michael Pollan teaches writing at the School of Journalism at the University of California at Berkeley. He is the author of* The Omnivore's Dilemma *(2006), a recent study of food politics and culture.*

Eat food. Not too much. Mostly plants.

That, more or less, is the short answer to the supposedly incredibly complicated and confusing question of what we humans should eat in order to be maximally healthy. I hate to give away the game right here at the beginning of a long essay, and I confess that I'm tempted to complicate matters in the interest of keeping things going for a few thousand more words. I'll try to resist but will go ahead and add a couple more details to flesh out the advice. Like: A little meat won't kill you, though it's better approached as a side dish than as a main. And you're much better off eating whole fresh foods than processed food products. That's what I mean by the recommendation to eat "food." Once, food was all you could eat, but today there are lots of other edible foodlike substances in the supermarket. These novel products of food science often come in packages festooned with health claims, which brings me to a related rule of thumb: if you're concerned about your health, you should probably avoid food products that make health claims. Why? Because a health claim on a food product is a good indication that it's not really food, and food is what you want to eat.

Uh-oh. Things are suddenly sounding a little more complicated, aren't they? Sorry. But that's how it goes as soon as you try to get to the bottom of the whole vexing question of food and health. Before long, a dense cloud bank of confusion moves in. Sooner or later, everything solid you thought you knew about the links between diet and health gets blown away in the gust of the latest study. . . .

## From Foods to Nutrients

It was in the 1980s that food began disappearing from the American supermarket, gradually to be replaced by "nutrients," which are not the same thing. Where once the familiar names of recognizable comestibles—things like eggs or breakfast cereal or cookies—claimed pride of place on the brightly colored packages crowding the aisles, now new terms like "fiber" and "cholesterol" and "saturated fat" rose to large-type prominence. More important than mere foods, the presence or absence of these invisible substances was now generally believed to confer health benefits on their eaters. Foods by comparison were coarse, old-fashioned and decidedly unscientific things—who could say what was in them, really? But nutrients—those chemical compounds and minerals in foods that nutritionists have deemed important to health—gleamed with the promise of scientific certainty; eat more of the right ones, fewer of the wrong, and you would live longer and avoid chronic diseases. . . .

*In the case of nutritionism, the widely shared but unexamined assumption is that the key to understanding food is indeed the nutrient.*

No single event marked the shift from eating food to eating nutrients, though in retrospect a little-noticed political dust-up in Washington in 1977 seems to have helped propel American food culture down this dimly lighted path. Responding to an alarming increase in chronic diseases linked to diet—including heart disease, cancer, and diabetes—a Senate Select Committee on Nutrition, headed by George McGovern, held hearings on the problem and prepared what by all rights should have been an uncontroversial document called "Dietary Goals for the United States." The committee learned that while traditional diets based largely on plants had strikingly low rates of chronic disease. Epidemiologists [medical professionals who assess the incidence and frequency of disease among large population] also had observed that in America during the war years, when meat and dairy products were strictly rationed, the rate of heart disease temporarily plummeted.

Naïvely putting two and two together, the committee drafted a straightforward set of dietary guidelines calling on Americans to cut down on red meat and dairy products. Within weeks a firestorm, emanating from the red-meat and dairy industries, engulfed the committee, and Senator McGovern (who had a great many cattle ranchers among his South Dakota constituents) was forced to beat a retreat. The committee's recommendations were hastily rewritten. Plain talk about food—the committee had advised Americans to actually "reduce consumption of meat"—was replaced by artful compromise: "Choose meats, poultry, and fish that will reduce saturated-fat intake." . . .

Henceforth, government dietary guidelines would shun plain talk about whole foods, each of which has its trade association on Capitol Hill, and would instead arrive clothed in scientific euphemism and speaking of nutrients, entities that few Americans really understood but that lack powerful lobbies in Washington. This was precisely the tack taken by the National Academy of Sciences when it issued its landmark report on diet and cancer in 1982. Organized nutrient by nutrient in a way guaranteed to offend no food group, it codified the official new dietary language. Industry and media followed suit, and terms like polyunsaturated, cholesterol, monounsaturated, carbohydrate, fiber, polyphenols, amino acids, and carotenes soon colonized much of the cultural space previously occupied by the tangible substance formerly known as food. The Age of Nutritionism had arrived.

## The Rise of Nutritionism

The first thing to understand about nutritionism—I first encountered the term in the work of an Australian sociologist of science named Gyorgy Scrinis—is that it is not quite the same as nutrition. As the "ism" suggests, it is not a scientific subject but an ideology. Ideologies are ways of organizing large swaths of life and experience under a set of shared but unexamined assumptions. This quality makes an ideology particularly hard to see, at least while it's exerting its hold on your culture. A reigning ideology is a little like the weather, all pervasive and virtually inescapable. Still, we can try.

In the case of nutritionism, the widely shared but unexamined assumption is that the key to understanding food is indeed the nutrient. From this basic premise flow several others. Since nutrients, as compared with foods, are invisible and therefore slightly mysterious, it falls to the scientists (and to the journalists through whom the scientists speak) to explain the hidden reality of foods to us. To enter a world in which you dine on unseen nutrients, you need lots of expert help.

---

*The most healthful foods in the supermarket sit there quietly in the produce section, silent as stroke victims.*

---

But expert help to do what, exactly? This brings us to another unexamined assumption: that the whole point of eating is to maintain and promote bodily health. Hippocrates's famous injunction to "let food be thy medicine" is ritually invoked to support this notion. I'll leave the premise alone for now, except to point out that it is not shared by all cultures and that the experience of these other cultures suggests that, paradoxically, viewing food as being about things other than bodily health—like pleasure, say, or socializing—makes people no less healthy; indeed, there's some reason to believe that it may make them more healthy. This is what we usually have in mind when we speak of the "French paradox"—the fact that a population that eats all sorts of unhealthful nutrients is in many ways healthier than we Americans are. So there is at least a question as to whether nutritionism is actually any good for you.

Another potentially serious weakness of nutritionist ideology is that it has trouble discerning qualitative distinctions between foods. So fish, beef, and chicken through the nutritionists' lens become mere delivery systems for varying quantities of fats and proteins and whatever other nutrients are on their scope. Similarly, any qualitative distinctions between processed foods and whole foods disappear when your focus is on quantifying the nutrients they contain (or, more precisely, the known nutrients).

This is a great boon for manufacturers of processed food, and it helps explain why they have been so happy to get with the nutritionism program. In the years following McGovern's capitulation and the 1982 National Academy report, the food industry set about re-engineering thousands of popular food products to contain more of the nutrients that science and government had deemed the good ones and less of the bad, and by the late '80s a golden era of food science was upon us. The Year of Eating Oat Bran—also known as 1988—served as a kind of coming-out party for the food scientists, who succeeded in getting the material into nearly every processed food sold in America. Oat bran's moment on the dietary stage didn't last long, but the pattern had been established, and every few years since then a new oat bran has taken its turn under the marketing lights. (Here comes omega-3!)

By comparison, the typical real food has more trouble competing under the rules of nutritionism, if only because something like a banana or an avocado can't easily change its nutritional stripes (though rest assured the genetic engineers are hard at work on the problem). So far, at least, you can't put oat bran in a banana. So depending on the reigning nutritional orthodoxy, the avocado might be either a high-fat food to be avoided (Old Think) or a food high in monounsaturated fat to be embraced (New Think). The fate of each whole food rises and falls with every change in the nutritional weather, while the processed foods are simply reformulated. That's why when the Atkins mania hit the food industry, bread and pasta were given a quick redesign (dialing back the carbs; boosting the protein), while the poor unreconstructed potatoes and carrots were left out in the cold.

Of course it's also a lot easier to slap a health claim on a box of sugary cereal than on a potato or carrot, with the perverse result that the most healthful foods in the supermarket sit there quietly in the produce section, silent as stroke victims, while a few aisles over, the Cocoa Puffs and Lucky Charms are screaming about their newfound whole-grain goodness. . . .

## Bad Science

But if nutritionism leads to a kind of false consciousness in the mind of the eater, the ideology can just as easily mislead the scientist. Most nutritional science involves studying one nutrient at a time, an approach that even nutritionists who do it will tell you is deeply flawed. "The problem with nutrient-by-nutrient nutrition science," points out Marion Nestle, the New York University nutritionist, "is that it takes the nutrient out of the context of food, the food out of the context of diet, and the diet out of the context of lifestyle."

If nutritional scientists know this, why do they do it anyway? Because a nutrient bias is built into the way science is done: scientists need individual variables they can isolate. Yet even the simplest food is a hopelessly complex thing to study, a virtual wilderness of chemical compounds, many of which exist in complex and dynamic relation to one another, and all of which together are in the process of changing from one state to another. So if you're a nutritional scientist, you do the only thing you can do, given the tools at your disposal: break the thing down into its component parts and study those one by one, even if that means ignoring complex interactions and contexts, as well as the fact that the whole may be more than, or just different from, the sum of its parts. This is what we mean by reductionist science.

Scientific reductionism is an undeniably powerful tool, but it can mislead us too, especially when applied to something as complex as, on the one side, a food, and on the other, a human eater. It encourages us to take a mechanistic view of that transaction: put in this nutrient; get out that physiological result. Yet people differ in important ways. Some populations can metabolize sugars better than others; depending on your evolutionary heritage, you may or may not be able to digest the lactose in milk. The specific ecology of your intestines helps determine how efficiently you digest what you eat, so that the same input of 100 calories may yield more or less energy depending on the proportion of Firmicutes and Bacteroidetes living in your gut. There is nothing very machinelike about the human eater, and so to think of food as simply fuel is wrong.

Also, people don't eat nutrients, they eat foods, and foods can behave very differently than the nutrients they contain. Researchers have long believed, based on epidemiological comparisons of different populations, that a diet high in fruits and vegetables confers some protection against cancer. So naturally they ask, What nutrients in those plant foods are responsible for that effect? One hypothesis is that the antioxidants in fresh produce—compounds like beta carotene, lycopene, vitamin E, etc.—are the X factor. It makes good sense: these molecules (which plants produce to protect themselves from the highly reactive oxygen atoms produced in photosynthesis) vanquish the free radicals in our bodies, which can damage DNA and initiate cancers. At least that's how it seems to work in the test tube. Yet as soon as you remove these useful molecules from the context of the whole foods they're found in, as we've done in creating antioxidant supplements, they don't work at all. Indeed, in the case of beta carotene ingested as a supplement, scientists have discovered that it actually increases the risk of certain cancers. Big oops. . . .

## The Elephant in the Room

In the end, the biggest, most ambitious and widely reported studies of diet and health leave more or less undisturbed the main features of the Western diet: lots of meat and processed foods, lots of added fat and sugar, lots of everything—except fruits, vegetables, and whole grains. In keeping with the nutritionism paradigm and the limits of reductionist science, the researchers fiddle with single nutrients as best they can, but the populations they recruit and study are typical American eaters doing what typical American eaters do: trying to eat a little less of this nutrient, a little more of that, depending on the latest thinking. (One problem with the control groups in these studies is that they too are exposed to nutritional fads in the culture, so over time their eating habits come to more closely resemble the habits of the intervention group.) It should not surprise us that the findings of such research would be so equivocal and confusing.

But what about the elephant in the room—the Western diet? It might be useful, in the midst of our deepening confusion about nutrition, to review what we do know about diet and health. What we know is that people who eat the way we do in America today suffer much higher rates of cancer, heart disease, diabetes, and obesity than people eating more traditional diets. (Four of the 10 leading killers in America are linked to diet.) Further, we know that simply by moving to America, people from nations with low rates of these "diseases of affluence" will quickly acquire them. Nutritionism by and large takes the Western diet as a given, seeking to moderate its most deleterious effects by isolating the bad nutrients in it—things like fat, sugar, salt—and encouraging the public and the food industry to limit them. But after several decades of nutrient-based health advice, rates of cancer and heart disease in the U.S. have declined only slightly (mortality from heart disease is down since the '50s, but this is mainly because of improved treatment), and rates of obesity and diabetes have soared.

No one likes to admit that his or her best efforts at understanding and solving a problem have actually made the problem worse, but that's exactly what has happened in the case of nutritionism. Scientists operating with the best of intentions, using the best tools at their disposal, have taught us to look at food in a way that has diminished our pleasure in eating it while doing little or nothing to improve our health. Perhaps what we need now is a broader, less reductive view of what food is, one that is at once more ecological and cultural. What would happen, for example, if we were to start thinking about food as less of a thing and more of a relationship? . . .

---

*The Western diet, with its 17,000 new food products every year, [leaves us] relying on science and journalism and marketing to help us decide questions about what to eat.*

---

## Food Science Ignores Food Culture

The last important change wrought by the Western diet is not, strictly speaking, ecological. But the industrialization of our food that we call the Western diet is systematically destroying traditional food cultures. Before the modern food era—and before nutritionism—people relied for guidance about what to eat on their national or ethnic or regional cultures. We think of culture as a set of beliefs and practices to help mediate our relationship to other people, but of course culture (at least before the rise of science) has also played a critical role in helping mediate people's relationship to nature. Eating being a big part of that relationship, cultures have had a great deal to say about what and how and why and when and how much we should eat. Of course when it comes to food, culture is really just a fancy word for Mom, the figure who typically passes on the food ways of the group—food ways that, although they were never "designed" to optimize health (we have many reasons to eat the way we do), would not have endured if they did not keep eaters alive and well.

The sheer novelty and glamour of the Western diet, with its 17,000 new food products introduced every year, and the marketing muscle used to sell these products, has overwhelmed the force of tradition and left us where we now find ourselves relying on science and journalism and marketing to help us decide questions about what to eat. Nutritionism, which arose to help us better deal with the problems of the Western diet, has largely been co-opted by it, used by the industry to sell more food and to undermine the authority of traditional ways of eating. You would not have read this far into this article if your food culture were intact and healthy; you would simply eat the way your parents and grandparents and great-grandparents taught you to eat. The question is, Are we better off with these new authorities than we were with the traditional authorities they supplanted? The answer by now should be clear.

It might be argued that, at this point in history, we should simply accept that fast food is our food culture. Over time, people will get used to eating this way and our health will improve. But for natural selection to help populations adapt to the Western diet, we'd have to be prepared to let those whom

it sickens die. That's not what we're doing. Rather, we're turn-
ing to the health-care industry to help us "adapt." Medicine is
learning how to keep alive the people whom the Western diet
is making sick. It's gotten good at extending the lives of people
with heart disease, and now it's working on obesity and diabetes. Capitalism is itself marvelously adaptive, able to turn the
problems it creates into lucrative business opportunities: diet
pills, heart-bypass operations, insulin pumps, bariatric sur-
gery. But while fast food may be good business for the healthcare industry, surely the cost to society—estimated at more
than $200 billion a year in diet-related health-care costs—is
unsustainable.

# The Government's Food Stamp Program Encourages Poor Eating

*Patt Morrison*

*Patt Morrison is a staff columnist for the* Los Angeles Times.

L OSE WEIGHT *on $3 a day! Ask me how!*

I'll tell you how: By living on food stamps. I did it, existing on a dollar-a-meal food-stamp allowance for a few days, and yeah, I lost a couple of pounds. But I don't advise it.

In the long run, it takes money to eat thin *and* healthy. For $3 a day—which is what you get when you divide 30 days into the $155 monthly food stamp allowance for one person—you wind up on the fatty-salty-sugary-canned-processed-bottled diet. *Get heart disease on $3 a day! Ask the government how!*

**FOR THE RECORD:**

Food stamps: Patt Morrison's May 24 column about taking the California Assn. at Food Banks' "food stamp challenge" used the wrong figure as the basis for the challenge's $3-a-day food allowance. The allowance is not based on a monthly food stamp allotment of $155, as the column indicated, but on a monthly allotment of $86. The maximum monthly food stamp allowance for an individual is $155; the average allotment for an individual is $86.

## The Food Stamp Challenge

Most e-mail come-ons I get invite me to split a dead man's unclaimed fortune in Nigeria, but this one, from the Bay Area–based California Assn. of Food Banks, offered me the "food stamp challenge." Could I tough it out eating on $3 a day? The association said 26 million Americans do—1,327,000 of them California children.

---

*Walk into a market with just $3 to spend for a day's menu and you'll shop with different eyes—and a different stomach.*

---

Well, I wasn't going to have some little kid bust my chops.

Could it be *that* hard? My father climbed electric poles for a living. We were thrifty; my mother sometimes served "special treat" pancake suppers that I found out years later were "special" because there was nothing else to eat before payday.

Still, we had a garden, my grandparents had a farm and my grandmothers "put up" food. Now I'd be going it alone—cold Tofurkey. But Tofurkey is, what, $2 a package? That's two-thirds of a day's budget for soy lunch meat! Already my thinking was shifting.

## What Three Dollars a Day Buys

Walk into a market with just $3 to spend for a day's menu and you'll shop with different eyes—and a different stomach. You veer away from the fresh and perishable to the filling and cheap, with a long shelf life. Letting anything spoil when you can't replace it is criminal—and unaffordable. As for staples, the bigger size almost always saves money but costs more up front. Anything organic or fresh or lower salt or lower fat almost certainly costs more than the processed stuff.

---

*Several members of Congress took the food stamp challenge, and now. . .[they're] trying to make the food stamp fund a little bigger.*

---

So I steered my cart past the produce—in some inner-city markets it's easier to find a bottle of beer than an apple—past the fresh juice and, with my mouth literally watering, stopped in front of bottled Asian sauces. Ordinarily I wouldn't look at them twice, but knowing they were off limits made them exotic and desirable. I also stopped at the glass freezer doors. They might as well have been museum cases for all that anyone could afford what was inside.

I did buy a little 3.25-ounce bottle of bacon-flavored soy bits for, I think, $1.29. At the *[Los Angeles] Times'* cafeteria I could get a tomato-and-spinach sandwich for 97 cents and sprinkle on the bits to make a faux BLT. With a glass of tap water, that's five lunches for a little over a buck each—I could skimp on dinner.

But not breakfast, my favorite meal. I found a loaf of the kind of bread that's mostly good for food fights—marked down from $2.19 to 99 cents. Yogurt, ten for $5. Even on sale, organic cage-free eggs are $3 a dozen, $1 more than the house brand from caged, chemical-fed hens. I usually drink a couple of gallons a week of nonfat organic milk, but that's $10— nearly half of my entire food allowance. Coffee was out of the question; a teabag, I could dip twice.

Two cans of high-protein, high-fiber black beans cost more than five of goopy, fatty refried beans. With corn tortillas and a pound of cheese—on sale for $3—and 10 14.5-ounce cans of diced tomatoes for $10 (compared to $2.29 for 16 ounces for fresh), I could have tostadas. Every . . . single . . . night.

The alternative? Hormel single-serving mac and cheese, 25% saturated fat and 820 milligrams of sodium. Cup Noodles, twelve for $4, but nearly half a day's sodium allotment in one serving. On a diet like that, I'd turn into Lot's wife—Lot's very fat wife.

## Congress May Act

Several members of Congress took the food stamp challenge, and now two of them, a Missouri Republican and a Massachusetts Democrats are trying to make the food stamp fund a little bigger and to guarantee that combat-zone pay doesn't knock military families off the food stamp eligibility list (yes, there are food stamp debit cards in the pockets of U.S. military uniforms).

## Class Matters

Sulking, hungry, I was planning a trip to the 99¢ Only store when I had a Holly Golightly inspiration. I dressed like I belonged in 90210 [the zip code for Beverly Hills] and sallied off to a high-end gourmet market. I bought a cup of real coffee for $1.25, plus 10 cents tax—a little over my $1 breakfast budget. (But wait—as I poured in milk and sugar, I saw little packets of tartar sauce and mayonnaise and Grey Poupon mustard—hallelujah, free condiments!)

With coffee in hand, I slipped a basket over my arm, dropped in a couple of random items and began strolling the store. Try the new tapenades? Why, thanks. Gosh, I just don't know which is better—could I try them both again? I sampled my way through several cheeses—I preferred the Irish cheddar—some walnuts in honey, fresh pineapple, a flavored crispbread ($5.29 for 5.3 ounces, a dollar an ounce, if I'd purchased it).

I decided not to buy anything—I was too full. Finally.

# CHAPTER 2

# Is the U.S. Food Supply Safe?

# Chapter Preface

In a statement released July 31, 2007, the U.S. Food and Drug Administration (FDA) announced a new set of standards for food inspectors with the purported goal being to "strengthen safety of food facilities overseen by states." The regulations apply to inspectors of food manufacturing, packaging, and processing facilities that are under the FDA's jurisdiction, and though recommended, the standards are not mandatory. While some may view this development as big government encroaching on state's rights, the bolstering of food safety is one issue that most will not argue against.

Different states currently impose regulations using various methods to ensure food safety based on the individual state's requirements. The FDA maintains that such inconsistent inspections make overarching regulation difficult, and ultimately create a risk of food-borne illnesses as well as workplace injuries. In addition, the FDA hopes that operating with one set of accepted standards may aid that administration in its regulation of manufactured food.

But critics argue that these standards, though they sound harmless, could result in burdensome paperwork that detracts from more important activities. The new standards call for documenting self-assessments, as well as completing forms to determine if a state meets the new criteria. Although some of this may result in safer food, some experts contend that the time spent filling out forms could be better spent on activities related to actual monitoring. Time and resources may be pulled away from results-specific tasks in order to comply with the new standards.

Lack of resources is certainly a concern of many critics of the FDA. With an estimated twenty million shipments of food coming into the United States each day, and only 450 inspectors responsible for checking those shipments, increased standards may not do enough to bolster the safety of the food supply.

Yet with continued outbreaks of serious food-borne illnesses such as *E. coli* and *salmonella,* and the announcement in July 2007 of contaminated meat that resulted in several cases of botulism [a paralytic disease caused by food-borne bacteria] the FDA may be looking for a way to increase its success at monitoring the food supply. The standards put forth by the FDA could be seen as acknowledgement of a need to work with states that hasn't been met in the past—whether due to a lack in funds or resources. Ensuring that all states operate under the same set of standards could result in fewer instances of contaminated food entering the national food supply.

The authors of the viewpoints in the following chapter discuss the issue of food safety. Some challenge new processing techniques, while others point to the need for increased regulations and enforcement of those regulations. While food safety is clearly important, the methods to ensure this safety can be debated. With resources often stretched thin, it is important that regulators research the best methods for ensuring the safety of the U.S. food supply.

# Irradiation and Genetically Modified Foods Increase Food Safety

*Henry I. Miller*

*Henry I. Miller is a physician and a fellow at the Hoover Institution, a public policy research center at Stanford University.*

Food poisoning from food contaminated with microorganisms is very common: 76 *million* cases and 5,000 deaths annually in the United States, according to government figures.

A couple of recent outbreaks have garnered a lot of attention. During [fall 2006], there have been three deaths and approximately two hundred cases of illness from *E. coli* O157:H7 [a harmful strain of *E. coli* bacteria commonly associated with undercooked ground beef and raw foods] (traced to fresh, bagged spinach), and about two hundred illnesses caused by *salmonella typhimurium* [a bacteria that causes food poisoning].

Federal officials investigating the spinach outbreak have narrowed their search to a handful of ranches in California's Salinas Valley and appear to be focusing on wild hogs as the cause of contamination. The source of the *salmonella* contamination is as yet unknown.

Americans are wondering who will protect us from future outbreaks of contamination and food-borne illness.

## Can Food-Borne Illness Be Prevented?

First, it's clear we can't rely on growers of fresh produce to protect us 100 percent of the time. Modern farming operations—especially the larger ones—already employ strict stan-

Henry I. Miller, "How to Make Our Food Safer," *TCS Daily, TechCentralStation*, November 6, 2006, www.tcs.com.supersizecon.html. Reproduced by permission.

dards and safeguards designed to keep food free of pathogens. And most often they work: Americans' food is not only the least expensive, but also the safest, in the history of humankind.

However, there is a limit to how safe we can make agriculture, given that it is an outdoor activity and subject to all manner of unpredictable challenges. If the goal is to make a field 100 percent safe from contamination, the only solution that guarantees this is to pave it over and build a parking lot on it. But we'd only be trading very rare agricultural mishaps for fender-benders.

It has also become painfully clear that we can't rely on processors to remove the pathogens from food in every case. This most recent outbreak of illness demonstrated that our faith in processor labels such as "triple washed" and "ready to eat" must be tempered with at least a little skepticism. Processors were quick to proclaim the cleanliness of their own operations and deflect blame toward growers. But all of those in the food chain share responsibility for food safety and quality.

---

*The technology that affords [organic growers] the best method of safeguarding their customers is the one they've fought hardest to forestall and confound.*

---

In fairness to processors, there is ample evidence to suggest that no amount of washing will rid all pathogens from produce. The reason is that the contamination may occur not *on* the plant, but *in* it. Exposure to *E. coli* or other microorganism, at key stages of the growing process may allow them to be taken into the plant and actually incorporated into cells.

## Irradiation Improves the Safety of Foods

Citing this, advocates of food irradiation [the process of subjecting foods to short-wave radiation in order to kill pathogenic bacteria, sterilize food, and increase shelf life] have stepped forward to claim that their technology can provide the assurance consumers demand and deserve. To be sure, irradiation is an important tool to promote food safety and is vastly under-used, largely due to opposition from the organic food lobby and government over-regulation.

But irradiation is no panacea. Although it quite neatly kills the bacteria, it does not inactivate the potent toxins secreted by certain bacteria such as *staphylococcus aureus* and *Clostridium botulinum*. This is a distinction you'd keenly appreciate should you become infected.

So, if consumers can't be protected by growers or processors or even irradiation, what can protect them?

## Genetically Modified Organisms Offer Additional Safety

There is technology available today that can inhibit microorganisms' ability to grow within plant cells and block the synthesis of the bacterial toxins. This same technology can be employed to produce antibodies that can be administered to infected patients to neutralize the toxins, and can even be used to produce therapeutic proteins that are safe and effective treatments for diarrhea, the primary symptom of food poisoning.

But don't expect your favorite organic producer to embrace this triple-threat technology, even if it would keep his customers from getting sick. Why? The technology in question is biotechnology [methods to alter genetic characteristics in foods for resistance to disease and pesticides, faster growth, or longer shelf life], or gene-splicing—an advance the organic lobby has vilified and rejected at every turn.

For organic marketers, the irony is more bitter than fresh-picked radicchio. The technology that affords them the best method of safeguarding their customers is the one they've fought hardest to forestall and confound.

Perhaps in the wake of at least three deaths and four hundred illnesses from the recent *E. coli* and *salmonella typhimurium* outbreaks, the organic lobby will rethink its opposition to biotechnology. Perhaps they will undertake a meaningful examination of the ways in which this technology can save lives and advance their industry.

I'm not betting the farm on it. After all, admitting you're wrong is hard. Blaming others is easy.

# New Food Technologies Are Safer than Older Ones

*Thomas R. DeGregori*

*Thomas R. DeGregori, PhD, is a professor of economics at the University of Houston and author of* Origins of the Organic Agriculture Debate.

Those critics who complain about the dangers of modern food production (such as "carcinogenic chemicals") are often the first to thwart efforts to make our food even better, safer, and more abundant through such new technologies as rBST [a growth hormone that increases a dairy cow's milk production], rDNA [artificial DNA created by combining or inserting one or more DNA strands], or irradiation [the process of subjecting foods to short-wave radiation in order to kill pathogenic bacteria, sterilize food, and increase shelf life].

One is reluctant to fault the consumer—who feels the food supply is pretty safe as is—for being concerned about the alleged dangers of transgenic [biotechnology that combines the genes of two organisms] food production. When the media attempt to be "balanced" and present "both sides" on such an issue—even though one side has no demonstrated competence—it is understandable that the public errs on the side of avoiding what they see as a small possibility of harm. Modern techniques of genetic engineering sound a bit daring and even "unnatural" (whatever that means), so the anti-biotechnology zealots have been able to play on fears of unknown and unknowable future harm. Since no reputable scientist can give a 100 percent certain guarantee against all unforeseen harm, the ideologue is free to sow the seeds of fear with little substantive challenge.

Thomas R. DeGregori, "20 Questions for Foodphobes," *American Council on Science and Health*, February 24, 2004. Reproduced with permission of American Council on Science and Health (ACSH). For more information on ACSH visit www.acsh.org.

## Twenty Questions about Improving the Safety of Food Crops

Rather than lecturing people about the technology that has made their food crops possible, and how easily old technologies, too, could be made to sound scary were we not all by now familiar with [them] I am trying an alternate strategy asking people twenty questions—some of which may sound scary—that I hope will make them think more rationally about food safety. Try to answer honestly, as you would without looking at the answers:

*Q: Would you favor mutation breeding using carcinogenic chemicals or gamma rays, or techniques such as altering the ploidy or chromosomal structure that allows the crossing of diploids [an organism with two sets of homologous chromosomes] and haploids [an organism having one of each homologous chromosome]?*

A: Well, this practice has been carried out in agricultural breeding since the 1920s.

*Q: Would you favor plant breeding tissue culture or somoclonal variation [genetic variation that results from tissue culture and regeneration], creating a plant from a cell in a cultured medium?*

A: It has been possible to do so since the late 1930s and has become increasingly important in plant breeding, particularly for disease resistance, since the late 1970s.

*Q: If a breeding technique is used that produces sterile crosses for plants that would otherwise not be able to produce a viable embryo, would you favor a procedure called embryo rescue to remove an embryo before it would naturally abort and then growing it in a cultured medium?*

A: It has been done for decades.

*Q: Would you favor a process called protoplastic cell fusion, a technique for removing the membrane of two cells and forcing the remaining protoplasm together, thereby fostering a gene transfer?*

A: Same as the previous answer.

Q: *Would you favor creating plant lines and irregular pheno-types [observable properties of an organism] that persist for some time not only in the original crop but in future crops in which they are part or the breeding stock and are difficult to eliminate by backcrossing?*

A: Avoid eating plant foods produced by tissue culture and embryo rescue.

Q: *Would you want to eat food products whose breeding pro-duced "unintended consequences" such as squash that caused food poisoning, a pest-resistant celery variety that produce rushes in agricultural workers (and was subsequently found to contain seven times more carcinogenic psoralens than control celery), or a potato variety that contained very high levels of toxic solanine [poisonous substance derived from potato sprouts, tomatoes, and nightshade]?*

A: These were all the products of traditional plant breed-ing and were noted by Codex Alimentarius [an internationally devised and supported set of standards for food process-ing]—in a meeting searching for the possible "unintended consequences" of rDNA, though none had yet been observed. The Lenape potato was promoted as an excellent new variety for producing better chips, but this product of (conventional) cross-breeding produced potentially deadly levels of the gly-coalkaloid solanine.

Q: *Would you eat a "killer zucchini" with high levels of natural toxins (curcubitan) that resulted in several recorded cases of people being hospitalized with food poisoning?*

A: According to Life Sciences Network (2003), the "only food scare in recent history in New Zealand . . . stemmed from the farming methods of organic farmers and others who use unconventional farming practices. The levels of toxin ap-parently increased among zucchini growers who did not spray their crops against an infestation of aphids, since insect preda-tion is sometimes associated with increased levels of toxins in plants". There was a "clear link between increased toxin levels and older open-pollinating varieties of seeds". The "most likely cause of the build-up of toxins is a genetic weakness in older varieties".

*Q: How would you feel about pharmaceuticals and vitamins made by microorganisms whose ability to express the desired product has been greatly expanded (sometimes a hundredfold) using a variety of techniques, including recombinant DNA, to increase production capability?*

A: Sorry, that is the way that most of them are produced, including an increasing number of rDNA pharmaceuticals.

*Q: Or maybe "all-natural" foods are more to your liking, though that includes cheeses, beverages, and breads made with genetically-engineered enzymes, yeasts, and emulsifiers—would you perhaps like to wash the stuff away with detergents that contain genetically-engineered enzymes created to replace the phosphates that were polluting our rivers and streams?*

A: These are all exempted from labeling requirements by European regulators and have been increasingly important since the 1980s.

*Q: In addition to protoplast fusion, might you support incorporation of cms (cytoplasmic male sterility) without restorer genes, radiated mentor pollen, and mutation induction?*

A: These have been staples of organic food production, through some of the more purist believers now wish to ban them immediately or phase them out in a ten-year transition since cell techniques are so firmly embedded in conventional breeding that banning them would set organic farmers back twenty years and have dramatic economic consequences.

*Q: Can one avoid most of the techniques described above by eating "organic"?*

A: As many [scientists] have noted, these and other techniques are even more important for "organic" agriculture than for conventional, since organic attempts to use fewer pesticides and therefore requires more disease-resistant crops.

*Q: How would you like to eat about 10,000 different toxins for dinner today?*

A: If you don't wish to do so, best that you skip any meal you had planned. Plants are chemical factories and produce a variety of secondary metabolites, some of which are toxins used to protect the plant. In addition, fungal or other infestation not only induces the production of more plant toxins but themselves produce potentially deadly toxins, which can occur in the field or at various stages of post-harvest storage and distribution.

*Q: Can you avoid these toxins by going "organic"?*

A: Quite the contrary. By being less well protected, organically grown plants are likely to produce more toxins. Since World War II, there has been a decline in stomach cancers, which many attribute to the use of fungicides in agriculture and refrigeration, reducing the need to use nitrates for meat preservation.

*Q: Are you willing to consume a variety of unintended impurities in your dinner such as aphids, rodent hair fragments, or animal excreta?*

A: Every food safety regulatory agency will have tolerance levels for these impurities. Modern food production and distribution technology greatly lowers these and other impurities but has yet to eliminate them totally. The best that one can say is that our ancestors ate far more contaminated food.

*Q: Does the possibility of the routine introduction of a large number of new plant varieties into the food chain disturb you?*

A: According to the National Research Council (1989), "Extensive experience has been gained from the routine introduction of plants modified by classical genetic methods. For example, an individual corn, soybean, wheat, or potato breeder may introduce into the field 50,000 genotypes [new experimental varieties] per year on average or 2,000,000 in a career.

Hundreds of millions of filed introductions of new plant genotypes have been made by American plant breeders in this century."

*Q: Would you feel all right about eating foods with large amounts of goitrogenic [produces a swelling of the thyroid gland] and estrogenically-active [a substance in which a natural steroid is operating] isoflavones [bioactive organic compounds found in plants] (the so-called endocrine [a hormone] disrupters)?*

A: If not, hold that tofu!

*Q: Would you want to eat food crops that had been protected by lead arsenate as a pesticide or the alkaloid nicotine, copper acetoarsenite, potassium 4,6-dinitro-o-cresylate, lime sulfurspray, hydrogen cyanide, sodium arsenite, and potassium antimonyl tartate?*

A: Your ancestors did before modern synthetic pesticides. Paris Green—copper aceto arsenite, a combination of copper acetate-$Cu(C2H2O2)$ and arsenic trioxide-$3Cu(AsO2)$—was as even more widely used as a pesticide in agriculture and for mosquito control. Other arsenic compounds were also used, such as London Purple, a by-product of the dye industry. Rachel Carson in *Silent Spring* compares the "endless stream of synthetic insecticides" to the "simpler inorganic insecticides" of pre-World War II days. The older insecticides were "derived from naturally-occurring minerals and plant products, compounds of arsenic, copper, lead, manganese, zinc and other minerals, pyrethrum from dried leaves of chrysanthemums, nicotine sulfate from some of the relatives of tobacco."

*Q: How would you react to the use in agriculture of a solution of inorganic salts, called Bordeaux mixture, even though the copper (often in the form of copper oxychloride or copper sulphate and lime) in it is toxic at the levels used? Or what about the use of sulfur, methaldehyde, and derris (rotenone, $CH23H22O6$), which was originally derived from the roots of a vine from tropical Asia?*

A: If you want to avoid it, you can't eat "organic."

*Q: Anyone for eating a food product that is the most likely to be contaminated with E. coli 0157:H7 and salmonella? The Emerging Infections Program of the Centers for Disease Control estimated that 20,000 people in North America contracted salmonella from consuming this food product in 1995.*

A: Hold those raw alfalfa sprouts, as there is no certain way of eliminating contaminants except by irradiation, which is unacceptable to the purists. In addition, alfalfa sprouts contain a highly toxic substance called canavine.

*Q: Do you believe that popular herbs, such as Echinacea purpura, St. John's Wort, Ginko biloba, ephedra, or the Chinese herbal products containing aristolochia acid are safe because they are somehow hallowed by tradition?*

A: Think again! Echinacea purpura is one of the few substances to which a person may have an adverse allergenic response on first contact. Echinacea is a member of the ragweed family. The data supports the "possibility that cross-reactivity between echinacea and other environmental allergens may trigger allergenic reactions in 'echinacea-naive' subjects" according to Raymond Mullins and Robert Heddle in their 2004 *Annals of Allergy, Asthma, & Immunology* article. Aristolochia acid, touted by some herbalists, has been shown to cause cancer and kidney failure according to Leslie Papp of the *Toronto Star*, nearly a hundred women with kidney damage from Chinese herbs at a "Belgian slimming clinic" were studied and several were found "in dire need of kidney transplants" and, "even worse," many of them were developing cancers in the kidney and bladder, years after taking the drug.

# New Biotechnologies Increase the Safety and Availability of Food Crops

*Gregory Conko*

*Gregory Conko is director of food safety policy at the Competitive Enterprise Institute, a pro-market, pro-limited government public-policy group.*

Ever since the publication of Rachel Carson's *Silent Spring*, environmental activists have warned of a slowly developing but widespread ecological catastrophe stemming from humankind's release of synthetic chemicals into the environment—particularly, the use of insecticides, herbicides, and fertilizers. Although the misuse of agricultural chemicals can have negative environmental impacts, fears that those chemicals would produce ecological catastrophe have proven unfounded. More importantly, any attempt to go without those chemicals would have meant sacrificing tremendous productivity gains and having to bring new, undeveloped land into agriculture.

What if similar benefits could be gained without such a heavy dependence on chemicals? Today, a new crop protection revolution is underway, and it is helping farmers combat pests and pathogens while reducing humanity's dependence upon agricultural chemicals. Biotechnology has made tremendous progress in transferring useful traits from one organism to another, allowing plants to better protect themselves from insects, weeds, and diseases.

The benefits have been so great that farmers have made bioengineered seeds perhaps the most quickly adopted agricultural technology in history. By 2002, just seven years after their introduction on the market, some 5.5 million farmers in more than a dozen countries planted over 145 million acres with gene-spliced crops. That year, 34 percent of all corn, 71 percent of all upland cotton, and 75 percent of all soybeans grown in the United States were bioengineered varieties. Biotech corn, cotton, and soybean have increased yields, reduced agricultural chemical use, and saved growers time, resources, and money. The increased productivity made possible by those advances allows farmers to grow substantially more food and fiber on less land. And each of those benefits helps to lighten agriculture's environmental footprint. . . .

---

*By most measures, organic farming is, in fact, more environmentally destructive than either conventional agriculture or the biotech alternative.*

---

## Risk

While it cannot be claimed that modified crops pose no risks to the environment, it is important that those risks be put into perspective. The threat posed by any plant—bioengineered, conventionally bred, or wild—has solely to do with the traits it expresses. Risk has nothing to do with how, or even if, a plant was modified. Countless scientific bodies, including the National Academy of Sciences, the American Medical Association, and others, have concluded that gene-splicing techniques themselves are actually safer than traditional breeding methods because breeders know which new genes are being added to plants and exactly what function those genes perform. Thus, bioengineered varieties are less likely, not more likely, to pose environmental or human health risks than are conventionally bred plants with similar traits. Critics of biotechnology, however, use out-of-context scare stories about such risks to argue for increasing the regulation of bioengineered crops across the board, regardless of the level of risk individual varieties may pose.

# Benefits

Risk aside, no examination of biotechnology would be complete without also considering the benefits such crops can deliver. After all, if the goal of regulation is to improve environmental health, we have to determine what benefits will be sacrificed when new products are delayed in reaching the market or made more costly by the regulation in question. Numerous human health benefits from bioengineered crops are on the horizon and a few have already been realized. However, most of the benefits that have already been delivered by gene-spliced plants are environmental. Since 1996, bioengineered crops have reduced agricultural chemical use, including insecticides and herbicides. Several varieties, nearly ready for market, will also help to reduce fertilizer use. Other products could increase agricultural productivity by allowing crop plants to better resist plant diseases or tolerate extremes of heat, cold, and drought.

Of course, many critics of modern industrial agriculture argue that the choice between biotechnology on the one hand and agricultural chemicals on the other poses a false dichotomy. They argue that organic production methods offer a more environmentally sensitive alternative to both systems. However, concluding that organic farming is better for the environment can only be done by ignoring the environmental costs imposed by organic methods. By most measures, organic farming is, in fact, more environmentally destructive than either conventional agriculture or the biotech alternative.

---

*Up to 40 percent of yield potential in Africa and Asia . . . is lost to insect pests and pathogens.*

---

# Pest Resistance

The use of agricultural chemicals is an environmental paradox. On the one hand, the runoff of agricultural chemicals into wetlands, streams, and lakes, as well as seepage of those chemicals into groundwater, can pose environmental problems. Overuse of chemical pesticides, for example, can damage biodiversity in areas adjacent to fields and kill fish or other important aquatic animals, insects, and plants. Overuse can even harm agricultural productivity itself by killing beneficial insects such as bees, other pollinators, and pest-eating insects in and around the fields. On the other hand, the failure to use such products means low productivity, which has its own adverse environmental impacts.

---

*[Chinese] farmers who planted only [genetically modified] varieties reported just one-sixth as many pesticide poisonings as those who planted only conventional cotton.*

---

It is estimated that up to 40 percent of yield potential in Africa and Asia, and about 20 percent in the industrialized world, is lost to insect pests and pathogens despite the ongoing use of copious amounts of pesticides. One benefit of agricultural biotechnology that has already been demonstrated is its ability to help better control insect pests, weeds, and pathogens. Among the most prevalent first generation products of agricultural biotechnology have been crop varieties resistant to chewing insects. That pest-resistance trait was added by inserting a gene from the common soil bacterium *Bacillus thuringiensis* (Bt) into the DNA of crop plants. Bt produces proteins that are toxic to certain insects, but not to mammals, fish, birds, or other animals, including humans. The bacterial proteins occur naturally, and foresters and organic farmers have cultivated Bt spores as a "natural pesticide" for decades, so it was an obvious choice for investigation by genetic engineers. Today, more than a dozen varieties of corn, cotton, and potato with the Bt protein trait have been commercialized.

## Corn—A Success Story

Consider the success of commercialized Bt corn in protecting plants from a range of chewing pests such as the European corn borer, a caterpillar pest that destroys an estimated $1 to $2 billion worth of corn each year. Caterpillars are difficult to control because they actually bore into stalks and ears of corn where they escape exposure to sprays. The Bt trait has provided farmers with the first truly effective means of controlling such infestations. Bt field corn varieties contributed to a modest reduction in insecticide use and increased yields by between three and nine percent, depending upon the intensity of infestation in a given year. Bt sweet corn has reduced insecticide use by between 42 and 84 percent. And Bt potato varieties cut pesticide applications by about half. In 2000, though, McDonald's and Burger King restaurants bowed to activist pressures and told their french-fry suppliers to stop using engineered potatoes, so the varieties were removed from the market the following year. . . .

Such a large reduction in synthetic insecticide use also saves resources that otherwise would be used in pesticide application. Economists from Louisiana State University and Auburn University found that, in the year 2000 alone, farmers planting Bt cotton varieties saved 3.4 million pounds of raw materials and 1.4 million pounds of fuel oil in the manufacture and distribution of synthetic insecticides, while 2.16 million pounds of industrial waste were eliminated. On the user end, farmers were spared 2.4 million gallons of fuel, 93 million gallons of water, and some 41,000 ten-hour days needed to apply pesticide sprays. Similar figures could easily be calculated for other bioengineered crops as well.

In less developed nations where pesticides typically are sprayed on crops by hand, use of Bt crops has even greater benefits. In China for example, some 400 to 500 farmers die every year from acute pesticide poisoning. Since the 1997 introduction of Bt cotton varieties in China, farmers reduced the quantity of pesticides applied to cotton by more than 75 percent compared to conventional varieties. As a direct consequence, farmers who planted only Bt varieties reported just one-sixth as many pesticide poisonings per capita as those who planted only conventional cotton. Smallholder farmers in the KwaZulu-Natal province of South Africa have achieved similar productivity and resource savings. . . .

## Weed Management

Among the most popular traits included in commercial bioengineered crop plants is herbicide tolerance. That feature allows farmers to apply a specific chemical herbicide spray over fields without damaging the growing crop. The trait has been developed in some plants with conventional breeding methods, but the process is more efficient and effective with gene-splicing techniques. Varieties of canola, corn, cotton, flax, rice, and sugar beet have all been bioengineered to tolerate herbicides, but by far the most popular herbicide-tolerant crop plant is Monsanto's Roundup Ready soybean. Planted on over 70 percent of all soybean acres in the United States, this variety is resistant to Monsanto's proprietary glyphosate herbicide, Roundup.

Farmers growing glyphosate-tolerant soybeans have realized herbicide cost savings and a significant reduction in the number of soybean herbicide treatments, although yields have not increased. The exact change in herbicide use varies among regions and growers, ranging from increases of as much as seven percent to reductions of up to 40 percent. Overall, the adoption of Roundup Ready soybeans has led to a modest net reduction in herbicide use. Nevertheless, adoption of those varieties accelerated a shift from relatively more harmful herbicides to glyphosate, which is generally considered an "environmentally friendly" chemical because it degrades quickly and has an extremely low toxicity. . . .

# The Organic Alternative

Organic and other "natural" farming advocates believe that intensive agriculture, which relies upon heavy use of synthetic and other "off-farm" inputs, devastates soil health, makes for unhealthy food of poor quality and taste, and has serious detrimental impact on the surrounding environment.

Yet claims that organic farming is a nearer and dearer friend to the environment are difficult to substantiate because organic practices merely trade some environmental threats for others. For example, organic farms do not use synthetic chemicals, but they do still need to control pests, weeds, and pathogens. Instead of synthetic pesticides, organic farmers use mineral- or plant-derived chemicals—including copper sulfate, pyrethrum, ryania, and sabadilla—to control insects and plant diseases. Yet, ounce for ounce, most of those chemicals are at least as toxic or carcinogenic as many of the newest synthetic chemical pesticides. Pyrethrum, for example, has been classified as a "likely human carcinogen" by a U.S. Environmental Protection Agency scientific panel. . . .

Productivity from organic farming and ranching is substantially lower than from conventional intensive agriculture. Organic farming generates yields that are at least five to 10 percent lower than conventional crop production and as much as 30 to 40 percent lower for important staple crops such as potatoes, wheat, and rye. Organic livestock productivity is approximately 10 to 20 percent lower than conventional husbandry. Even those yield drags can be misleading because soil nutrient replacement on organic farms requires lands to be fallowed with nitrogen-fixing plants such as clover or alfalfa for two or three years in every five or six. Conventional farming that incorporates soluble mineral fertilizers does not need to fallow land. Thus, conventional farms can achieve total yields per acre that are as much as 40 to 100 percent greater than organic farms. Alternatively, they can match the yields of organic farms with only 50 to 70 percent of the land.

## The Importance of Productivity

The importance of agricultural productivity for ecological stewardship and habitat conservation should be evident. The loss and fragmentation of native habitats caused by agricultural development, along with the conversion of both wilderness areas and agricultural lands into residential areas, are widely recognized as among the most serious threats to biodiversity. According to a recent report published by Future Harvest and IUCN/The World Conservation Union, "reducing habitat destruction by increasing agricultural productivity and sustainability" is one of the six most effective ways to preserve wildlife biodiversity.

Over the past 50 years, the world's population doubled from three billion to six billion, and it is expected to grow by an additional three billion in the next half-century. Fortunately, over the past five decades, the development of better plant varieties and animal breeds, and the production and better use of herbicides, pesticides, fertilizers, and other agronomic technologies—collectively known as the "Green Revolution"—dramatically increased per-acre agricultural yields. That is perhaps the most remarkable environmental success story in history.

---

*We have to place [biotechnologies'] risks and benefits into a broader context that does not ignore the risks posed by conventional and organic production.*

---

From 1961 to 1993, the earth's population increased 80 percent, but cropland increased only eight percent, all while per-capita food supplies rose. Higher food demand was met almost totally by increasing per-acre yields. Had that not been the case and agricultural productivity in 1993 remained at the 1961 level, producing the same amount of food would have required increasing the amount of cropland and grazing land by 80 percent or more. In other words, an additional 27 percent of the world's land area (excluding Antarctica) would have had to come into agricultural use. Surely, that would be an environmental nightmare far greater than any of those imagined by opponents of agricultural technology.

Still, similar yield increases will be necessary in the twenty-first century if the projected population is to be fed with an equally light impact on the environment. The projected increase in food demand can be supplied in one of two ways: increasing the land area dedicated to agriculture or increasing agricultural productivity. Though the ability of conventional technology to increase agricultural productivity over the past few decades has been impressive, it is not guaranteed to continue. Annual increases in agricultural productivity have been declining in recent years. Cereal yields per hectare rose 2.2 percent per year in the late 1960s and 1970s, but only 1.5 percent per year in the 1980s and early 1990s, and as little as just 1.0 percent by the end of the '90s. Consequently, some scientists believe new breakthroughs will have to come from bioengineering techniques. Fortunately, biotechnology is much more flexible, precise, and powerful than those earlier methods of genetic manipulation, and rapid productivity gains of 5, 10, and even 25 percent in individual varieties from a single added trait are not unrealistic. . . .

## Threats to the New Biotechnologies

. . . The biggest threat bioengineered plants face is overly restrictive policies based on the false notion that there is something inherently dangerous about biotechnology. Of course, not all the products of gene-splicing will prove to be better than the best conventional ones. Some will have inferior agronomic [field-crop production and soil management] properties; others may express traits that pose genuine environmental or human health risks. But to gauge the value of individual applications or agricultural biotechnology as a whole, we have to place their risks and benefits into a broader context that does not ignore the risks posed by conventional and organic production practices or our ability to manage those risks responsibly. Yet that is exactly how advocates of increased regulation would have us examine them: without reference to the place biotechnology occupies in the broader spectrum of plant modification and other agricultural practices.

Numerous attempts have been made in recent years to increase the regulatory burden borne by the products of biotechnology—through both agency rulemaking and congressional legislation. All of those attempts have two things in common: They require regulators to consider only the risks of bioengineered crops and not their benefits, and they hold gene-splicing to a standard of safety that could not possibly be met by non-biotech products and practices. Heightened regulation of certain high-risk plant varieties may indeed be warranted. But the appropriate level of oversight cannot be achieved simply by singling out bioengineered varieties for differential treatment. When biotechnology is evaluated on a level playing field, farmers, consumers, and regulators will find that it outshines its competitors.

# Hormone Use in Dairy Cows Increases Milk Production and Is Safe

*John Fetro*

*John Fetrov ...duction*
*medicine a ...terinary*
*Medicine.*

Maybe ... Foods (ann ... llion in the U.S.) h ... r accept milk in sor ... m dairies that us ... [a synthesized ar ... that increases lac ... nilk] in their cows.

Given Dean Food's share of the market in the region (about 70 percent of milk) and, thus, its market dominance, its decision in effect requires dairy producers across New England to stop using a technology that is profitable, exhaustively researched and shown to be safe, has no effect on the milk Dean Foods processes and that has been very widely used across the U.S. dairy industry for more than a decade.

I rather suspect that some would say that the decision was in response to consumers who want to buy milk from cows not treated with rbST. I have no doubt that there are small numbers of consumers for whom rbST is an issue, since there has been a niche market for "milk from cows not treated with rbST" since the hormone was approved for use in the dairy industry.

John Fetrow, "Food Fear is Anti-bST Marketing Tool," *Center for Global Food Issues*, September 25, 2006. Reproduced by permission of www.feedstuffs.com.

## Fearmongering as a Marketing Strategy?

In my opinion, authentic consumer demand is not driving things here. Instead, I am suspicious that the choice may be part of a deliberate marketing strategy. It may be more plausible that Dean Foods decided that it could increase or defend its market share and/or command a markup in price with "rbST free" milk that it couldn't with "generic milk."

Market differentiation in any retail industry is nothing new. As consumers, we all are bombarded each day with products claiming to be different from the competition.

Designer perfumes command a higher price based on the glitz they can build around their brand, not what is really in the bottle. It was Mr. Revlon himself who said: "In the factory, Revlon manufactures cosmetics; in the store, we sell hope."

For perfume companies competing for a bit of people's disposable income, this is a pretty harmless game. With food, it is not. The truth is that milk from cows treated with rbST is the same as milk from cows not treated, but if you can create a fear in the public's mind that there is a dangerous difference, then you have a way to differentiate your product, capture market share, and charge more for the same milk.

*Determined and well-funded special interests and dominant corporate entities can . . . push out competition and charge more for what is really the same food.*

Other major food corporations, not to mention the organic food industry, have been using the power of first creating and then marketing "food fear" for some time.

One large corporation has been advertising "cholesterol-free corn oil," playing on consumer ignorance that no vegetable oil has cholesterol. Another major corporation advertised chicken with "no hormones and no steroids added" while knowing this was true of all chicken.

## *Hormone* as a Scare Word

The word "hormone" is really handy if you want to scare the average consumer. Never mind that such campaigns undermine the consumer's confidence in the generic product and add to consumer doubts about all food production. Never mind that in the case of rbST, there is no way to actually verify that the claim you make is really true. Never mind that the decision hurts the dairy producers that were profitably using an approved, well-established production technology in their herds.

In the Northeast in particular, where else were they going to go to sell their milk? Never mind that removing rbST from the industry will increase the cost of production to dairy producers and, ultimately, the price of dairy products to consumers. Never mind that removing rbST increases the dairy industry's impact on the environment. It is the processor's near-term volume and margin that matter here.

The dairy industry (and all food production industries) needs to understand that this is not really about rbST. It is just this moment's convenient target. This is about who will control the production and distribution of food. It is about whether determined and well-funded special interests and dominant corporate entities can partner with each other to push out competition and charge more for what is really the same food.

If this places irrelevant demands on producers, that's their problem. Dairy producers may shrug and say they can do without rbST. As they do so, they need to understand that there will be other targeted production technologies to follow, many with a weaker scientific base of evidence for safety, welfare or environmental impact.

## New Technologies Attacked as Unsafe

One can safely predict that this decision, taking advantage of deliberately generated "food fear," will be used by advocacy groups to build momentum as they attract donations and target whatever next production practice they decide to dislike for whatever self-interested reason.

Corporate interests will jump on the bandwagon in a greedy effort to capture some temporary advantage in the marketplace. More ill-conceived demands will be made of producers: rationality, science, practical impacts, environmental, and consumer costs not withstanding. The abundant, efficient, and cost-effective production of wholesome food for society will be the victim.

From my vantage, I can only say: "May your children live in the society you help create."

# Self-Regulation by the Food Industry Keeps Food Safer than Government Regulation Does

*Steve Chapman*

*Steve Chapman is a columnist for the* Chicago Tribune.

There are lots of theories on how to succeed in business. But here's one that never occurred to me: Poison your customers.

This strategy sounds counterintuitive, since the dead don't do much buying, but some people think it accounts for periodic outbreaks of food-borne illness. They say you can't trust the private sector to keep pathogens out of our food, making it incumbent on the federal government to protect us.

The recent episode of lethal pet food is Exhibit A in this case. Adulterated wheat flour made its way from China to factories in the United States and Canada that produce food for dogs and cats. The contamination killed or sickened thousands of animals and led to the recall of more than one hundred brands of pet food.

Many liberals insist the only remedy is more regulation. "If we expect to have our spinach uncontaminated, our pet food safe, Congress has to give the FDA more resources," says Donald Kennedy, former Commissioner of the Food and Drug Administration.

But this case also shows that, when a product goes wrong, everyone in the supply chain has a big stake in making it right. Chinese exporters stand to lose a vast amount of sales if they don't raise their safety standards. Pet-food makers will face rejection from retailers unless they can show their products pose no danger. Stores that continue to sell tainted goods will send their patrons to the competition.

No one wants poisoned food, and in the age of the Internet, bad news travels at the speed of light. A company invites disaster if it harms consumers. Customers can leave, and lawsuits can exact ruinous judgments.

---

*Does the private sector do a perfect job on food safety? Of course not—but no system created by human beings is infallible.*

---

After a 1993 *E. coli* epidemic caused by Jack in the Box hamburgers, the parent company had to pay tens of millions of dollars to victims. When Hudson Foods was implicated in a 1997 outbreak, it lost its biggest customer, Burger King, and soon had to sell out to rival Tyson Foods.

Major corporations like Kraft Foods and Nestle now make a priority of knowing where their ingredients come from and testing them for safety, reports *BusinessWeek*. ConAgra Foods, which had to recall Peter Pan peanut butter because of *salmonella*, spent $15 million to prevent a recurrence. After last year's outbreak of *E. coli* was traced to California spinach, handlers of leafy greens forged an agreement whose signatories must adopt tough sanitary practices—monitored with inspections that they pay for through voluntary assessments. Some 99 percent of the state's leafy greens are now covered.

Does the private sector do a perfect job on food safety? Of course not—but no system created by human beings is infallible. Government falls way short of perfection in all sorts of areas, whether it's leaving New Orleans vulnerable to hurricanes, operating crime-infested public housing projects, or building bridges to nowhere.

Those advocating a busier FDA take it for granted that more federal enforcement would mean safer food. But history offers few grounds for such faith.

In his new book, *Government Failure Versus Market Failure*, economist Clifford Winston of the Brookings Institution strongly questions the effectiveness of government safety regulation of workplaces, consumer products, and medicines. In all these areas, he says in an interview, "there is little evidence that 1) there's a major problem to be solved or 2) the government has significantly benefited consumers and workers."

One reason is that no government agency can monitor everything that needs monitoring. Food imports alone amount to 25,000 shipments every day. David Acheson, recently named to the new job of FDA commissioner for food protection, told the *Baltimore Sun*, "Right now, we inspect 1 percent of food imports. If we were to inspect 2 percent, would that problem go away? I don't think so."

Notwithstanding the relatively small federal role, Americans understand that the food supply is exceptionally safe. Even during an outbreak of food-borne illness, we continue to shop with great confidence. If *E. coli* is found in spinach, we assume we're safe eating hundreds of other foods—and with very few exceptions, we're right.

No surprise there. As the father of economics, Adam Smith, wrote in 1776, "It is not from the benevolence of the butcher, the brewer, or the baker that we expect our dinner, but from their regard to their own interest." Their own interest forces them to worry about safety, and that incentive is the best protection we could have.

# Food Safety Regulations and Lack of Enforcement Leave America's Food Supply Unsafe

*Paul Krugman*

*Paul Krugman is a columnist for the* New York Times *and teaches at the Woodrow Wilson School of Public and International Affairs at Princeton University in Princeton, New Jersey.*

Yesterday I did something risky: I ate a salad.

These are anxious days at the lunch table. For all you know, there may be *E. coli* on your spinach, *salmonella* [this and E. coli are bacteria that can cause food poisoning] in your peanut butter, and melamine in your pet's food and, because it was in the feed, in your chicken sandwich.

Who's responsible for the new fear of eating? Some blame globalization; some blame food-producing corporations; some blame the Bush administration. But I blame Milton Friedman.

## Globalization and the Food Supply

Now, those who blame globalization do have a point. U.S. officials can't inspect overseas food-processing plants without the permission of foreign governments—and since the Food and Drug Administration [FDA] has limited funds and manpower, it can inspect only a small percentage of imports. This leaves American consumers effectively dependent on the quality of foreign food-safety enforcement. And that's not a healthy place to be, especially when it comes to imports from China, where the state of food safety is roughly what it was in this country before the progressive movement.

The *Washington Post*, reviewing FDA documents, found that last month the agency detained shipments from China that included dried apples treated with carcinogenic [cancer-producing] chemicals and seafood "coated with putrefying bacteria." You can be sure that a lot of similarly unsafe and disgusting food ends up in American stomachs.

---

*The Bush administration won't issue food safety regulations even when the private sector wants them.*

---

## American Food Industry's Role in Food Safety

Those who blame corporations also have a point. In 2005, the FDA suspected that peanut butter produced by ConAgra, which sells the product under multiple brand names, might be contaminated with *salmonella*. According to the *New York Times*, "when agency inspectors went to the plant that made the peanut butter, the company acknowledged it had destroyed some product but declined to say why," and refused to let the inspectors examine its records without a written authorization.

According to the company, the agency never followed through. This brings us to our third villain, the [George W.] Bush administration (2001–2009).

## Government Inaction Spells Danger to Food Supply

Without question, America's food safety system has degenerated over the past six years. We don't know how many times concerns raised by FDA employees were ignored or soft-pedaled by their superiors. What we do know is that since 2001 the FDA has introduced no significant new food safety regulations except those mandated by Congress.

This isn't simply a matter of caving in to industry pressure. The Bush administration won't issue food safety regulations even when the private sector wants them. The president of the United Fresh Produce Association says that the industry's problems "can't be solved without strong mandatory federal regulations": Without such regulations, scrupulous growers and processors risk being undercut by competitors more willing to cut corners on food safety. Yet the administration refuses to do more than issue nonbinding guidelines.

---

*"E. coli conservatives" [are] ideologues who won't accept even the most compelling case for government regulation.*

---

## The Cost of Poor Regulation

Why would the administration refuse to regulate an industry that actually wants to be regulated? Officials may fear that they would create a precedent for public-interest regulation of other industries. But they are also influenced by an ideology that says business should never be regulated, no matter what.

The economic case for having the government enforce rules on food safety seems overwhelming. Consumers have no way of knowing whether the food they eat is contaminated, and in this case what you don't know can hurt or even kill you. But there are some people who refuse to accept that case, because it's ideologically inconvenient.

## Self-Interest Is a Poor Regulator

That's why I blame the food safety crisis on Milton Friedman, who called for the abolition of both the food and the drug sides of the FDA. What would protect the public from dangerous or ineffective drugs? "It's in the self-interest of pharmaceutical companies not to have these bad things," he insisted in a 1999 interview. He would presumably have applied the same logic to food safety (as he did to airline safety): regardless of circumstances, you can always trust the private sector to police itself.

O.K., I'm not saying that Mr. Friedman directly caused tainted spinach and poisonous peanut butter. But he did help to make our food less safe, by legitimizing what the historian Rick Perlstein calls "*E. coli* conservatives": ideologues who won't accept even the most compelling case for government regulation.

Earlier this month the administration named, you guessed it, a "food safety czar." But the food safety crisis isn't caused by the arrangement of the boxes on the organization chart. It's caused by the dominance within our government of a literally sickening ideology.

# New Technologies Supplant Old Precautions with High-Tech Shortcuts

## Marion Nestle

*Marion Nestle is the Paulette Goddard professor of nutrition, food studies, and public health at New York University. She is the author of* Food Politics *(2002),* Safe Food *(2003), and* What to Eat *(2006), and appeared in the movie* Super Size Me *(2004).*

As citizens, we need to understand that producing safe food is not impossibly difficult. Food scientists proved years ago that HACCPA-[Hazard Analysis and Critical Control Point, a system preventing pathogens from entering the food supply] systems prevented foodborne illness in outer space. Those systems should work just as well on earth. Sweden, Denmark, and the Netherlands have reduced foodborne illnesses by instituting control systems at every stage of production, starting on the farm. They set testing standards to reduce pathogens, limit antibiotics in animal feed, prevent infections in transported animals, test for microbes at slaughterhouses and supermarkets, and provide incentives to the industry to comply with safety rules. Our government could also take such actions. That it does not is a result of an entrenched political system that allows federal regulators to avoid enforcing their own rules, and food companies to deny responsibility and blame each other, the regulators, or the public whenever outbreaks occur. Rather than collaborating to reduce foodborne pathogens, the agencies and companies shift attention to consumer education as the best way to ensure safe food. Failing that, they call for foods to be irradiated or pasteurized.

This [article] examines the education, irradiation, and pasteurizarion alternatives along with two others: using the courts to impose legal liability for foodborne illness, and reorganizing government to consolidate and improve oversight of food safety. . . .

## The FDA: Food Safety Is an Individual Responsibility

When it comes to food safety, the public bears all of the health risks. But does that mean that we also must bear the entire burden of preventive measures? Of course, home cooks should follow basic principles of food safety, especially because doing so is not difficult and is almost always effective. Cooking kills most microbial pathogens, and cooked food remains relatively free of them when refrigerated or stored properly. Surveys, however, frequently find that home cooking practices violate the FDA's [Food and Drug Administration] manual of food safety rules, the *Food Code*. This should be no surprise; hardly anyone has heard of it. Furthermore, the code is easy to violate; one merely needs to wipe a counter with an old sponge, use a dish towel more than once, store fresh and cooked foods on the same refrigerator shelf, or forget to wash hands. Even so, home code violations cause much less illness than those made by out-of-home food preparers who did not follow food safety rules.

Nevertheless, addressing food safety in the home is now a primary goal of national public health policy. In 1980, when the Department of Health and Human Services (DHHS) established its first ten-year plan to improve health practices, officials estimated that nearly 75 percent of foodborne infections originated in restaurants, institutional food services, or processing plants. The plan mentioned washing hands and proper food handling as useful educational measures for workers in the food industry. Ten years later, DHHS assigned home cooks their own food safety objective: "Increase to at least 75 percent the proportion of households in which principal food preparers routinely refrain from leaving perishable food out of the refrigerator for over two hours and wash cutting boards and utensils with soap after contact with raw meat and poultry: (Baseline: for refrigeration of perishable foods, 70 percent; for washing cutting boards with soap, 66 percent; and for washing utensils with soap, 55 percent, in 1988)." This meant that by the year 2000, 75 percent of home cooks should be routinely washing cutting boards with soap, as compared to 66 percent in 1988. The 1988 baseline figures indicated that a sizable-proportion of the population *already* followed safe food-handling practices fairly often—or at least said they did.

In 2000, with foodborne infections increasing in frequency and severity, DHHS assigned an entire section to food safety in its ten-year plan for 2010. The overall goal, to *reduce foodborne illnesses*, includes three objectives dealing with pathogens—reduce infections, reduce outbreaks, and prevent antibiotic-resistant salmonella [bacterium]. Another objective calls for an increase to 79 percent in "the proportion of consumers who follow key food safety practices." Because baseline data from a 1998 survey confirmed that 72 percent of consumers already did so, the goal recognizes that home code violations are not the principal cause of outbreaks. For this reason, DHHS added a "developmental" objective—one for which no baseline information is available—to "improve food employee behaviors and food preparation practices that directly relate to foodborne illnesses in retail food establishments." Taken together, these objectives continue to place the responsibility for food safety on food handlers, not on food producers or processors.

The phrase *key food safety practices* refers to elements of an education campaign jointly organized by the USDA [United States Department of Agriculture] and DHHS through an entity called the Partnership for Food Safety Education, an "am-

-

bitious public-private partnership created to reduce the incidence of foodborne illness by educating Americans about safe food handling practices." . . .

---

*Labor issues affect food safety because they lead to unsafe handling practices[:]. . . washing hands infrequently, staying on the job while sick. . .*

---

## Commercial Food Handlers Are Poorly Regulated

Although the advice given in such campaigns makes perfect sense, the education alternative hardly appears adequate to deal with problems of food safety, especially when focused exclusively or primarily on consumers. Scientifically based or not, the educational programs of the partnership, the USDA, and food corporations are directed toward a minor source of foodborne illness at the very end of the food chain (If anything, food producers, processors, and servers are the groups most in need of education about food safety.) If, for example, meat and poultry producers better understood their role in the safety of the food supply, they might be less hostile and more receptive to the value of Pathogen Reduction: HACCP. They might understand why it is so important to institute healthier working conditions and more comprehensive training programs for employees. . . . Food handlers typically earn the minimum wage, receive no sick leave health benefits, and may not have obtained much education. Many workers in meat and poultry processing plants are illegal immigrants with even less access than others to such benefits. These labor issues affect food safety because they lead to unsafe handling practices such as washing hands infrequently, staying on the job while sick, and failing to obtain treatment for intestinal infections. Education of employees would help, but education alone is not enough to ensure safe food. If we as a society are serious about preventing foodborne illness, we need to make certain that everyone who handles food is educated, is paid adequately, and, when needed, obtains sick leave and health care.

---

*The sterility induced by irradiation . . . is usually incomplete and temporary. The food must be irradiated in intact packages.*

---

## Irradiation Is Not the Answer

Because regulatory approaches to food safety are endlessly obstructed, and educational approaches do not address underlying causes, the food industry and some health officials urge more immediate action: irradiate foods to kill pathogens.

. . . Irradiation kills unwanted microbes. It uses the elements cobalt-60 and cesium-137 or electric current as sources of gamma rays, x-rays, or electron beams to bombard foods. These rays disrupt the genetic material (DNA) of cells in proportion to the intensity of the source element and the length of exposure. Lower or shorter bouts of radiation reduce the number of microbes on a food; higher and longer exposures can kill all of them.

Contrary to the belief of some critics, irradiation does not cause the foods themselves to become radioactive, and its physical effects on food are not so different from those induced by cooking (which also disrupts cell structures). High-intensity irradiation induces minor losses of nutrients as well as slight changes in color, flavor, and odor, particularly in fatty meats. Whether these changes matter depends on point of view. Proponents of irradiation view taste disadvantages as minor in comparison to the ravages of *E. coli* O157:H7 [a rare strain of *E. coli* that can cause severe discomfort and death]. From the perspective of science-based risk assessment, the benefits of food irradiation far outweigh taste considerations.

The sterility induced by irradiation, however, is usually incomplete and temporary. The foods must be irradiated in intact packages; once the packages are opened or damaged, foods can become recontaminated. Thus, irradiated foods must be handled like fresh foods and may need to be refrigerated to retard bacterial growth. Even so, this process confers substantial advantages to food producers and processors. They no longer need to be concerned about *preventing* contamination, because irradiation takes care of whatever pathogens are present. It also extends shelf life; irradiated strawberries, for example, can last 22 days on the shelf instead of the usual 3 to 5 days.

Despite such advantages, the process is highly controversial and has been slow to gain acceptance. The very idea of irradiation induces dread and outrage, not least because it involves radiation, a foreign and personally uncontrollable technology. It also cannot guarantee sterility, and it treats rather than prevents safety problems. At best, irradiation is an end-stage technological fix. . . .

In the early 1960s, the FDA began to authorize irradiation for limited use, one food at a time: first wheat and wheat flour; then spices, dried vegetable seasonings, pork, and chicken products for the general public; and then steak and turkey for astronauts. In turn, the USDA authorized irradiation for pork, poultry, and beef. Both agencies work to expand this list. In 2002, for example, the USDA proposed to permit Hawaii to export irradiated peppers, eggplants, mangoes, pineapples, squash, and tomatoes to the mainland. Overall, more than thirty-five countries have approved irradiation as a means to preserve more than fifty different kinds of foods. Numerous national and international organizations have endorsed the process, among them health and food technology associations and—most enthusiastically—groups representing irradiation companies.

In the United States, the FDA requires irradiated foods to be labeled "treated with (or by) radiation" and to display the international symbol of irradiation—the radura—printed in green. . . .

## Commercial Irradiation
## Finds Market Support

Because fears of public disapproval inhibited development of the irradiation industry, the first multipurpose commercial food plant did not open until 1991. In 1994, Isomedix, a New Jersey company with sixteen plants that irradiate medical devices and food packaging materials, petitioned the FDA to authorize irradiation of raw beef and lamb. Cattlemen strongly supported the petition and discussed the matter with their friends in Congress. Congress, in turn, pressured the USDA and FDA to come to a rapid decision. In 1997, during the period when USDA Secretary Dan Glickman was attempting to convince the Senate agriculture committee that his department should be allowed to issue mandatory recalls of contaminated meat, the senators "reacted skeptically, saying the plan would impose unnecessary new regulations when the focus should be on emerging technology like irradiation."

---

*Fears of consumer resistance easily explain why the industry . . . pressed so forcefully for more attractive euphemisms [for irradiation].*

---

Other groups also advocated approval of irradiation, charging that opposition to it was antiscientific. . . .

The Produce Marketing Association, an industry trade group, also supported irradiation for reasons of both science *and* values, in this case the value of "consumer choice": "Sound science must be the basis for decisions about all food issues. . . . Irradiation has been deemed to be a safe and viable technology . . . providing consumers the choice in the marketplace." Such statements, as we have seen, mistakenly equate safety (a scientific concept) with acceptability (a social concept). Meat industry officials, while lobbying for approval of irradiation, wanted to make sure that using it would not increase their accountability for foodborne illness: "Irradiation

... is particularly important for ground beef ... but the ultimate responsibility for food safety still rests with the food handler and preparer."

## Congress Pressures the FDA to Authorize Irradiation

The FDA delayed approval of irradiation for beef and lamb, not only because its approval processes are always slow, but also because its staff still needed to evaluate the effects of the process on meat from sheep as well as cattle and on fresh cuts as well as those that had been refrigerated and frozen. While the FDA was plugging along on its proposals for these rules, Congress passed the Food and Drug Administration Modernization Act of 1997 which, among other things, restricted the agency's ability to regulate irradiated foods: "No provision ... shall be construed to require on the label or labeling of a food a separate radiation disclosure statement that is more prominent than the declaration of ingredients," and "FDA must act on petition within sixty days of enactment or provide to House and Senate an explanation of the process followed ... and the reasons action on the petition was delayed." Congress, therefore, insisted that the FDA allow food labels to disclose irradiation in very small type and approve irradiation requests within months rather than years.

Under that kind of pressure, the FDA immediately authorized irradiation of beef and lamb, explaining that the process "will not present a toxicological hazard, will not present a microbiological hazard, and will not adversely affect the nutritional adequacy of such products." The American Meat Institute hailed the approval as "a victory for consumers and the red meat industry."

## Hiding Irradiation from Consumers

Despite ... opposition, pressures to hide irradiation from consumers continued. In 2002, Congress passed the Farm Security and Rural Investment Act, mostly to authorize $190 billion in price supports for basic farm commodities, but also to equate irradiation (a radiation process) with pasteurization [using high temperatures to kill most of the pathogenic bacteria and viruses in the food] (usually understood as a heat process). The act requires the FDA to allow food labels to use *pasteurized* for any process that reduces pathogens in meat and poultry and to substitute this term for irradiation. This creative idea originated with Tom Harkin (Dem-IA), chair of the Senate agriculture committee, and a representative of the state housing the nation's largest irradiation plant for ground beef. Even with such legislation, it is not clear whether the public will accept irradiated foods. Some experts believe that people will simply refuse to buy irradiated products; this possibility makes food producers so nervous that they all "want to be second to try it." Some companies deliberately appeal to distrust of irradiation by advertising their products as nonirradiated. Fears of consumer resistance easily explain why the industry and its supporters pressed so forcefully for more attractive euphemisms such as "ionizing pasteurization" or "cold pasteurization." Will euphemisms convince people to buy irradiated products? Surveys reveal that at least half of consumers do not like *any* term for irradiation.

---

*Irradiation is expensive because of the equipment, the labels, and the transport from centralized facilities.*

---

Other surveys, however, report the public to be relatively unconcerned about this process, leading its proponents to reassure the food industry that consumers will readily accept irradiated foods. One report to industry (costing $75 a copy) promises readers that most consumers think irradiation will prevent foodborne illness and reduce disease risk (85–90 percent) and that most would buy irradiated products even if they were labeled as such (80 percent). The report quotes the president of the Food Marketing Institute: "Food irradiation is one safety tool whose time has come! . . . As an industry, we must also have the courage to support irradiated food products in the marketplace. . . . We must not let those who are afraid to let consumers make their own judgments use misinformation and scare tactics to win arguments they would lose on the scientific merits of the issues."

## Irradiation Increases Cost to Consumers

Cost considerations, however, are likely to influence levels of outrage about this method, as may euphemistic labels so small as to be unnoticeable. Food technologists believe that when informed of the benefits of irradiation, the public will buy treated foods even if they cost more, as they most certainly will. Irradiation is expensive because of the equipment, the labels, and the transport from centralized facilities; the higher costs will be passed along to consumers. In 1997, USDA economists estimated that the cost to the beef industry alone could range from $28 million to $89 million annually, or from about 1.6 cents to 5 cents a pound. Although the costs to society of foodborne illness greatly exceed such amounts, and the additional price seems too small to make any difference to individual consumers, market comparisons suggest that a 10 percent premium for irradiated products would cause the proportion of people who might choose them to drop from 43 percent to 19 percent. . . .

This experiment is now underway. As irradiated foods increasingly enter the marketplace, the degree of acceptance by industry and the public will soon become evident.

Like many other food safety matters, irradiation raises issues of societal values that extend beyond the scientific. To questions about costs and benefits must be added others about the safety of those employees who work with and transport hazardous radioactive materials, and the environmental effects of discarding surplus sources of gamma rays. From a value-based perspective, irradiation is a techno-fix: a short-term corrective to a late-stage contamination problem that should be addressed much earlier in the chain of production.

# New Technologies of Raising Animals Decrease Food Safety

## Eric Schlosser and Charles Wilson

*Eric Schlosser is the award-winning author of* Fast Food Nation *(2001), a study of the American fast-food industry. In 2006 he published* Chew on This, *an adaptation of* Fast Food Nation *for younger readers.*

Greeley, Colorado, is about 150 miles north of the Hanna Ranch. But it might as well be on another planet. You can smell Greeley long before you can see it. The smell is hard to forget but not easy to describe, a combination of live animals, manure, and dead animals being turned into dog food. Think of rotten eggs mixed with burning hair and stinky toilet, and you get the idea. The smell is worst during the summer months, blanketing Greeley day and night like an invisible fog. Many people who live there no longer notice the smell. It fades into the background, present but not present, like the sound of police sirens and honking horns when you're in New York City. Other people who live in Greeley can't stop thinking about the smell, even after years. It seeps into everything, gives them headaches, makes them nauseous, interferes with their sleep. Greeley is a modern-day factory town where cattle are the main units of production, where workers and machines turn big animals into small vacuum-sealed packages of meat.

The billions of fast-food hamburgers that Americans eat every year come from places like Greeley. The industrialization of cattle-raising and meatpacking over the past few decades has completely altered the way beef is produced—and the towns that produce it. Responding to the demands of the fast-food and supermarket chains, the meatpacking firms have cut their costs by cutting the wages of workers. They have turned one of the nation's best-paying factory jobs into one of the lowest-paying. They have recruited a workforce of poor immigrants who have little power and suffer terrible injuries on the job. The harms of this new meatpacking system are being felt not only by the workers employed by it but also by the animals processed by it—and by consumers who eat its meat. WELCOME TO GREELEY, a sign along the highway says: AN ALL-AMERICAN CITY.

---

*Slaughterhouse lagoons can be as big as twenty acres and as much as fifteen feet deep, filled with millions of gallons of really disgusting stuff.*

---

Swift & Co. runs one of the nation's meatpacking plants just a few miles north of downtown Greeley. Weld County, which includes Greeley, earns more money every year from livestock than any other county in the United States. Swift & Co. is the largest private employer in Weld County, running a beef slaughterhouse and a sheep slaughterhouse as well as processing facilities. Outside town, a pair of enormous feedlots supply the beef slaughterhouse with cattle. Each feedlot can hold up to 100,000 cattle. At times the animals are crowded so closely together it looks like a sea of cattle, a mooing, moving mass of brown-and-white fur that goes on for acres. These cattle don't wander the prairie, eating fresh grass. During the three months before slaughter, they eat special grain dumped into long concrete troughs that look like highway dividers. The grain is designed to fatten the cattle quickly, aided by growth hormones that have been implanted beneath their skin.

Male cattle that will be processed for their meat are called steers. A typical steer will eat almost 3,000 pounds of grain during its stay at a feedlot, just to gain 400 pounds in weight. The process involves a good deal of waste. Each steer deposits about 50 pounds of urine and manure every day. Unlike human waste, this stuff isn't sent to a treatment plant. It's dumped into pits—gigantic pools of pee and poop that the industry calls lagoons. Slaughterhouse lagoons can be as big as 20 acres and as much 15 feet deep, filled with millions of gallons of really disgusting stuff. As you might expect, the lagoons smell incredibly bad and sometimes they leak, sending raw sewage into nearby rivers and streams. In 1991 one billion fish were killed in North Carolina by a disease linked to the runoff from slaughterhouse lagoons. People had to use bulldozers to bury the dead fish. The amount of waste created by the cattle that pass through Weld County is staggering. The two big feedlots outside Greeley produce more pee and poop than the cities of Denver, Boston, Atlanta, and St. Louis—combined.

The smell from slaughterhouse lagoons isn't just unpleasant. It can also be harmful. The pools of waste emit various dangerous gases, including hydrogen sulfide and ammonia. Hydrogen sulfide—also known as "sewer gas" or "stink damp"—can be harmless in very small doses. Our own digestive system produces it: bad breath gets some of its bad smell from tiny amounts of hydrogen sulfide. Large concentrations of hydrogen sulfide can kill you (although nobody's breath has ever been that bad), and even small amounts, inhaled over a long period of time, can cause all kinds of health problems. Slaughterhouse lagoons release tons of hydrogen sulfide into the air. People who live nearby often complain about headaches, nausea, asthma, shortness of breath, and dizziness. Some studies suggest that breathing air polluted with hydrogen sulfide can cause permanent damage to the nervous system and the brain.

Farmers and ranchers have always used some of the manure from their animals as fertilizer. Putting manure on a field can be a good way to help crops grow. But no society in human history has ever had feedlots and slaughterhouses as big as the ones near Greeley. There have never been so many animals and so much manure in one place before. Strange things can happen when you don't watch out. In the fall of 2004, a pile of manure at a large feedlot in Milford, Nebraska, caught on fire. As manure decomposes, it gets hot and releases gases that burn easily, such as methane. If there's enough manure, it can catch on fire without anyone's lighting a match. Big manure fires are no longer unusual. At the Milford feedlot, once the 4-million-pound, 30-foot-high pile of manure started to burn, it was hard to put out. The local fire department tried twice, without success. When the owner flattened the pile with heavy equipment, the smoldering fire spread. Spraying a lot of water on it threatened to pollute nearby streams. The massive pile of poop burned for nearly four months, with smoke drifting from it for miles. . . .

---

*The ability of the meatpacking companies to avoid strict food-safety rules has been made possible by their close ties to members of Congress.*

---

A generation ago, the typical outbreak of food poisoning involved a small gathering: a church supper, a family picnic, a wedding reception. Contaminated food made a group of people in one local area get sick. Such traditional outbreaks still take place. But the nation's current system of food processing has created a whole new sort of outbreak, one that can potentially sicken millions of people.

The construction of huge feedlots, slaughterhouses, and hamburger grinders has made it easier for E. coli O157:H7 and other nasty germs to spread through the nation's food supply. In the 1970s there were thousands of small slaughterhouses in the United States. Today thirteen large slaughterhouses supply most of the beef eaten by almost 300 million

Americans. The meatpacking system that arose to supply the nation's fast-food chains—an entire industry molded to serve their needs, to provide gigantic amounts of uniform ground beef so that all McDonald's hamburgers would taste the same—has proven an extremely efficient system for spreading disease.

While medical researchers have pointed out the links between modern food processing and the rise in food poisoning, the nation's leading meatpacking companies have strongly opposed government efforts to pass tough food-safety laws. For years the meatpacking industry has managed to avoid the kind of rules that apply to the manufacturers of most consumer products. If a defective toy somehow poses a risk to small children—for example, if a piece could easily break off and be swallowed—the U.S. government can demand that every one of those toys be removed from stores. But the U.S. government cannot order a meatpacking company to remove contaminated, potentially lethal ground beef from fast-food kitchens and supermarkets—even if that meat can kill children. The government can't even fine companies that knowingly sell bad meat. "We can fine circuses for mistreating elephants," the head of the USDA once admitted, "but we can't fine companies that violate food-safety standards."

The ability of the meatpacking companies to avoid strict food-safety rules has been made possible by their close ties to members of Congress. Every year the industry gives millions of dollars to politicians who support its point of view. Meatpacking companies don't want people to get sick. But they also don't want to be held legally responsible when bad meat does make people sick. Being held legally responsible would require these companies to pay the medical bills of everyone sickened by their meat. The industry's attitude today is much the same as it was a hundred years ago, when a member of the beef trust told Congress why his company opposed the Meat Inspection Act of 1906. "There is no limit to the expense that might be put on us," he said. "In all reasonableness and fairness *we are paying all we care to pay.*"

The risk of contamination begins in the feedlot. Far from their natural habitat on the prairie, cattle in feedlots become prone to all sorts of illnesses. They get little exercise and live amid pools of manure. "You shouldn't eat dirty food and dirty water," a government health official says. "But we still think we can give animals dirty food and dirty water." Modern feedlots have become places where germs are easily spread from one animal to another. *E. coli* O157:H7 can live in cattle troughs and survive in cattle manure for up to ninety days.

The germs from infected cattle are spread not only in feedlots but also at slaughterhouses and hamburger grinders. The slaughterhouse tasks most likely to contaminate meat are the removal of an animal's furry hide and of its digestive system. If the hide hasn't been cleaned well, chunks of dirt and poop may fall from it onto the meat. The digestive system is still pulled out of cattle by hand. If the job is not performed carefully, the contents of the stomach and intestines may spill everywhere. The speed of today's production lines makes the task much more difficult. A single worker at a "gut table," may have to pull the guts out of sixty cattle every hour. Doing the job properly takes a fair amount of skill. Doing it wrong spills the stomach contents, full of germs, all over the meat. Knives are supposed to be cleaned and disinfected every few minutes, something that workers in a hurry tend to forget. A contaminated knife spreads germs to everything it touches. The faster the line, the more likely that people will make mistakes.

---

*A single fast-food hamburger now contains meat from hundreds or even thousands of different cattle.*

---

The risk of widespread contamination grows when the meat is turned into ground beef. A generation ago, local butchers made hamburger meat out of leftover scraps. Ground beef was sold locally, and it was often made from cattle slaughtered locally. Today enormous slaughterhouses and grinders dominate the production of ground beef. A modern plant can produce almost a million pounds of hamburger meat a day, shipping it throughout the United States and even overseas. A single animal infected with *E. coli* O:157:H7 can contaminate 32,000 pounds of that ground beef.

To make matters worse, the animals used to make about one quarter of the nation's ground beef—old dairy cattle—are those most likely to be sick and diseased. Dairy cows can live as long as forty years, but they are often slaughtered at the age of four, when their milk production starts to fall. McDonald's relies heavily on dairy cattle for its hamburger supplies, since the animals are relatively cheap and yield leaner meat. The days when hamburger meat was ground in the back of a little butcher shop, out of leftover scraps of beef, are long gone. The mixing together of meat from a large number of animals at ground beef plants has played a crucial role in spreading *E. coli* O157:H7. A single fast-food hamburger now contains meat from hundreds or even thousands of different cattle.

Children who eat ground beef must make sure that it has been completely cooked. It should be well done. There shouldn't be a single particle of meat that still looks pink. Cooking the meat thoroughly kills germs like *E. coli* O157:H7. But it doesn't change a rather unappetizing fact. There are all sorts of complicated scientific explanations for how germs are spread in feedlots, how germs are spread in slaughterhouses, how germs are spread in hamburger plants. Behind them lies a simple explanation for why eating a hamburger can now make you seriously ill: there is poop in the meat.

# Genetic Engineering Is Too Dangerous to Be Used in Human Foods

*Brian Tokar*

*Brian Tokar is a faculty member and biotechnology project director at the Institute for Social Ecology in Vermont and the author of* The Green Alternative *(1987, rev. 1992) and* Earth for Sale *(1997).*

**B**rian Tokar—Isn't GM [Genetically Modified food] just an extension of traditional breeding practices?

Luke Anderson, Dr. Michael Antoniou, and Professor Joe Cummins: No—GM bears no resemblance to traditional breeding techniques. The government's own Genetic Modification (Contained Use) Regulations admit this when it defines GM as "the altering of the genetic material in that organism in a way that does not occur naturally by mating or natural recombination or both."

Traditional breeding techniques operate within established natural boundaries which allow reproduction to take place only between closely related forms. Thus tomatoes can cross-pollinate with other tomatoes but not soya beans; cows can mate only with cows and not sheep. These genes in their natural groupings have been finely tuned to work harmoniously together by millions of years of evolution. Genetic engineering crosses genes between unrelated species which would never cross-breed in nature.

*Could this be dangerous?*

Potentially, yes. In one case, soya bean engineered with a gene from a brazil nut gave rise to allergic reactions in people sensitive to the nuts. Most genes being introduced into GM

"GM Food: A Guide for the Confused." Say No to GMOs, September 2006. www.saynotogmos.org/ud2006/usept06.php#confused.

plants have never been part of the food supply so we can't know if they are likely to be allergenic.

More seriously, in 1989 there was an outbreak of a new disease in the United States, contracted by over 5,000 people and traced back to a batch of L-tryptophan food supplement produced with GM bacteria. Even though it contained less than 0.1 percent of a highly toxic compound, 37 people died and 1,500 were left with permanent disabilities. More may have died, but the American Centers for Disease Control stopped counting in 1991.

The US government declared that it was not GM that was at fault but a failure in the purification process. However, the company concerned, Showa Denko, admitted that the low-level purification process had been used without ill effect in non-GM batches. Scientists at Showa Denko blame the GM process for producing traces of a potent new toxin. This new toxin had never been found in non-GM versions of the product. . . .

*Are GM foods more dangerous to allergy-prone people?*

The problem with GM foods is their unpredictability. A person may prove unexpectedly allergic to a food he has previously eaten safely. For this reason, people who are hyper-allergenic or environmentally sensitive may want to avoid GM foods. . . .

---

*Genes engineered into plants and animals can be transferred to other species. . . . Genes from GM oilseed rape [canola], salmon, or microorganisms may move into the gene pools of wild relatives.*

---

*What will the impact of GM crops be on the environment?*

Last year, 71 percent of all GM crops grown were genetically engineered to be herbicide resistant. A field can now be sprayed with chemicals and everything will die except for the resistant crop. The sales of one of the herbicides being used are predicted to rise by $200 million as a result.

Graham Wynne, Chief Executive of the Royal Society for the Protection of Birds, says: "The ability to clear fields of all weeds using powerful herbicides which can be sprayed onto GM herbicide-resistant crops will result in farmlands devoid of wildlife and will spell disaster for millions of already declining birds and plants."

There are also GM virus-resistant crops. Prof Joe Cummins says: "Probably the greatest threat from genetically altered crops is the insertion of modified virus and insect virus genes into crops—genetic recombination will create virulent new viruses from such constructions. The widely used cauliflower mosaic virus (present in the GM soy and maize [corn] currently on supermarket shelves in the UK) is a potentially dangerous gene. It is very similar to the Hepatitis B virus and related to HIV. Modified viruses could cause famine by destroying crops or cause human and animal diseases of tremendous power."

*What is genetic pollution?*

Genes engineered into plants and animals can be transferred to other species. For example, genes from GM oilseed rape [canola], salmon, or micro-organisms may move into the gene pools of wild relatives. The introduction of GM organisms into complex ecosystems may bring knock-on effects that we are unable to control.

---

*Scouts are sent around the world to discover genes that may have commercial applications.*

---

*Which foods are not GM?*

Presently certified organic foods are the best bet for the anti-GM consumer. However, even with the best intentions, companies attempting to exclude GM ingredients from their products have found contamination from GM crops. De Rit recently had to recall a batch of organic tortilla chips after tests showed that they contained GM maize [corn]. The company believes that cross-pollination of crops was to blame. Iceland, the only supermarket chain to try to ban GM ingredients from its own-brand products, recently wrote to its suppliers acknowledging that some GM contamination is unavoidable, because of cross-pollination of crops. The Linda McCartney range of vegetarian meals has also been discovered to be contaminated with GM soya.

Meanwhile, organic farming is under threat from the biotech companies. In the United States, lawyers from the biotech companies are trying to force the government to require that GM crops can be declared organic. Some U.S. states have succumbed to Monsanto's pressure and banned GM-free labels on food. Monsanto has successfully sued dairy farmers who labelled dairy products as free of Monsanto's genetically engineered bovine growth hormone.

Due to so-called free trade agreements established by the World Trade Organisation, it may become illegal for individual countries to maintain higher organic standards than the United States. So what happens in the United States has a direct knock-on effect on Europe.

*Why are genes being patented?*

Patents give a huge incentive to the biotechnology industry to create new GM organisms. Since most patents last for seventeen to twenty years, the companies are keen to recoup any investment quickly, often at the expense of safety and ethics. There are currently patents approved or pending for over 190 GM animals, including fish, cows, mice, and pigs. There are also patents on varieties of seeds and plants, as well as unusual genes and cell lines from indigenous peoples. Scouts are sent around the world to discover genes that may have commercial applications. Over half the world's plant and animal species live in the rainforests of the south and the industry has been quick to draw upon these resources.

The Neem tree, for instance, has been used for thousands of years in India for its antiseptic and insecticidal properties. Following in the well-trodden footsteps of Christopher Columbus, western corporations have filed a number of patents on these attributes.

# More Powerful Antibiotics in Dairy Cattle Increase the Likelihood of Drug-Resistant Bacteria Infecting Humans

*Minneapolis Star Tribune*

*Anonymous Editorial*

Wisconsin dairy farmer John Vrieze wants FDA [Food and Drug Administration] permission to give his cows a powerful antibiotic, cefquinome, that is now the drug of choice and last resort for several difficult-to-treat human conditions. He shouldn't get that permission. That would be, as the Gold'n Plump billboards say about antibiotics and animals, a "cock-a-doodle-don't."

By all accounts, Vrieze is a very good dairy farmer who embraces advanced techniques for keeping his cows happy, healthy, and producing. So when one of his cows comes down with bovine respiratory disease, he'd like to treat the animal with a powerful drug, cefquinome. The manufacturer of cefquinome has petitioned the Food and Drug Administration for permission to begin selling the drug for use in animal husbandry.

That has set up a tug of war between those opposed to wider use of antibiotics in animals and those who favor it. In this battle, the opponents are the good guys; they include the American Medical Association, other health groups, and the FDA's own advisory panel.

## FDA Drug Approval Would Make Humans More Vulnerable

The problem is that the disease-causing microbes which antibiotics attack constantly mutate. The wider the use of an antibiotic, the sooner one of those mutations will defeat the drug.

Widespread use of antibiotics in animals accelerates this process tremendously, leaving humans more vulnerable to diseases once controllable. That's what is behind a movement to reduce the use of antibiotics in animals, and why the Gold'n Plump billboard is an effective marketing device.

---

*FDA guidelines have been rewritten so that approval . . . is pretty much guaranteed unless opponents can prove a risk.*

---

Enter cefquinome. A close cousin, cefepime, is the only effective treatment available for some serious infections. Worried that using cefquinome in animals puts the efficacy of cefepime at risk the advisory board at the FDA's Center for Veterinary Medicine recommended against approving animal use.

The panel had two other reasons for voting the way it did: A dozen other, effective treatments already are on the market for bovine respiratory disease, and the incidence of that disease can be significantly reduced if the animals are treated right—i.e., not frequently moved long distances and not packed tightly together.

Notwithstanding the common-sense judgment that drugs from the cephalosporin family should be reserved for humans, the FDA may still approve it for animals. The reason is one that has become common under the Bush administration: deference to industry.

FDA guidelines have been rewritten so that approval in a case like this is pretty much guaranteed unless opponents can prove a risk to a drug used in humans to fight a food-borne illness. Since that is not the case for cefquinome, dairy farmer Vrieze may get his wish and be allowed to use its close cousin on his sick dairy cows. His "Bossy" may be better off, but someone's very sick Aunt Millie eventually is going to pay the price. Something's wrong with that outcome.

# CHAPTER 3

# Are Fast and Snack Foods Responsible for Obesity Among Youth?

# Wellness Programs Encompass Diet and Exercise

*Amanda Paulson*

*Amanda Paulson is a staff writer for* The Christian Science Monitor.

Erykah Martin's lunch is a model of nutrition: a lettuce and carrot salad, an apple, a granola bar, and (the one kid-like concession) chocolate milk.

Salad is the second-grader's favorite lunch item, she says, "'cause all the things you put in it is healthy and good." She wrinkles her nose and shakes her black braids at the idea of hot dogs, the cafeteria's hot lunch option that day.

## Promoting Healthy Choices

The salad bar at Chicago's Nettelhorst Elementary School, where Erykah goes, is one way the school is promoting healthier choices for students. It also teaches nutrition, has an after-school cooking program, has reinstituted recess, and has dance and physical education classes—the sorts of programs needed at far more schools, children's health advocates say, given the rise in childhood obesity.

The trends can seem alarming—one recent study showed that 17 percent of children and adolescents were overweight in 2004, up from 14 percent just five years earlier. But more and more, schools are starting to address the problem.

By summer [2006], they must meet a federal mandate for a comprehensive wellness plan. Recently introduced federal legislation would require new minimum nutrition standards for school lunches. Numerous states are passing laws aimed at better food and more physical activity for students. A few individual schools, like Nettelhorst, are also taking the initiative.

---

*Recently introduced federal legislation would require new minimum nutrition standards for school lunches.*

---

"I'm very encouraged by what is occurring in schools," says Kelly Brownell, director of the Rudd Center for Food Policy and Obesity at Yale University. "One can just see the landscape changing. . . . At the moment, it's still a minority of schools, but the number is growing and the state legislatures are getting involved in requiring schools to change."

## Obesity Is a Critical Issue

The problem, he and others agree, is critical. One recent New York study showed that one in four kids in the city's Head Start program was obese by the age of two and 40 percent of the Head Start kids were either obese or overweight. The Centers for Disease Control and Prevention doesn't have an "obese" designation for children. But its National Health and Nutrition Examination Survey—considered the gold standard of weight data because it uses actual measures instead of self-reporting—showed that 17 percent of children between ages two and nineteen were overweight in 2004. Another 17 percent were at risk of becoming so.

---

*Studies show that overweight children are highly likely to become obese adults.*

---

Studies show that overweight children are highly likely to become obese adults, who have an elevated risk of many health problems. And America's growing obesity rate is a prime reason for rapidly rising healthcare costs, health experts say.

## Legislators Focus on Schools

Schools have become the major legislative target for obvious reasons: Kids eat many meals there—often breakfast and lunch—and policy can regulate schools in a way that's impossible with families.

"Schools alone didn't cause the problem, and schools alone can't solve the problem, but we'd be hard-pressed to solve it without schools," says Howell Wechsler, director of the Division of Adolescent and School Health at the Centers for Disease Control.

A few reform advocates see particular promise in the wellness policies that all schools must have in place by the coming school year. "It really gives us an opportunity to have this discussion in a way that can get systemwide changes," says Alicia Moag-Stahlberg, director of Action for Healthy Kids, a national group that works with schools and is helping many create their wellness policies. "And kids have to be part of it, too. If you make changes to the school meal line without kids' involvement, you may just encourage more bootlegging out of the locker."

## Obesity Factors

The reasons for the obesity problem are varied: bigger portion sizes, kids who spend more time in front of TVs and video games, neighborhoods that aren't safe enough for outdoor play or walking or biking to school.

And experts say that school-nutrition guidelines are outdated. For example: jelly beans, lollipops, and breath mints are not allowed, but donuts, French fries, and soda are. Even more troubling is the food not sold in cafeterias.

"There is junk food for sale in just about every school in America," says Allison Dobson, a spokeswoman for Sen. Tom Harkin (D) of Iowa, who is sponsoring a bipartisan bill to change the standards and make them apply to all food in schools, including that in vending machines. "This is a time when we should be molding our kids' habits."

## Teaching Kids About Healthier Options

Critics of such bills—primarily the snack-food industry, but also some schools worried about losing revenue—often say kids won't eat healthier options.

"We feel that teaching kids to lead a balanced, healthy lifestyle and make smart choices is more important than restricting one category of food," says Jennifer Phillips, a spokesperson for the American Beverage Association. She notes that the ABA has adopted a voluntary policy that limits high school vending-machine options to 50 percent soft drinks, and supplies elementary schools only with water and 100 percent juice. "We think it should be a balance ... and more about teaching children about nutrition and exercise."

---

*"We think it should be a balance ... and more about teaching children about nutrition and exercise".*

---

But all that's needed may be a little creativity, says Christina Paxson, a Princeton University professor of public affairs and editor of a recent report on childhood obesity. Successful programs "engage kids in learning about healthy food, usually in very hands-on ways. They get them to help prepare the food instead of just lecturing them, they get them engaged in physical activity in fun ways, sometimes in unconventional non-gym-class ways."

## Kids Pick Salads, After a Little Teaching

That sort of engagement has worked at Nettelhorst, which was part of a pilot project that put salad bars in three Chicago elementary schools. A study of the project showed that without any nutrition education, few kids chose the salads; with education, the number doubled. On some days, nearly a third of Nettelhorst students choose salad. No junk food is available.

Susan Kurland, Nettelhorst's principal, also made the decision to bring back recess—a rarity in Chicago, where a recent survey showed just 6 percent of elementary schools have a recess of at least twenty minutes. "There isn't anything happening here that can't happen at any other school," she adds. "Somewhere along the way we lost the idea that school is where you teach kids how to live life."

# Snack Foods and School-Lunch Fast Foods Contribute to Childhood Obesity

*Greg Critser*

*Greg Critser is a regular contributor to* USA Today, *the* Los Angeles Times, *and* Harper's *magazine.*

In the 1980s, snacking was flat-out encouraged. The first to do so were the decade's ever more economically busy parents, who simply wanted to make sure that their kids ate *something*. Fair enough. But snacking was also indirectly encouraged by new understandings in nutritional science, which suggested that many people, and particularly children, needed to eat more than three meals a day. Although such insights have a strong basis in fact, their real-world utility was often twisted by the media and food companies. Suddenly it was "unnatural" to eat three times a day. Progressive people ate "when their bodies told them to." Snacking was not only not bad; it was good to eat all day long. Such was the message of the diet craze known as "grazing," a quasi-regimen endlessly fawned over and packaged by the mainstream media.

Food companies, of course, were happy to join in the party. There would be "Snack Good," "Snack Healthy," and, by the early 1990s, "SnackWell." And with sugar and fat prices lower than ever, it was easy for new, less bridled players to share the fun and profit. The number and variety of high-calorie snack foods and sweets soared; where all through the 1960s and 1970s the number of yearly new candy and snack products remained stable—at about 250 a year—that number jumped to about 1000 by the mid-1980s and to about 2000 by the late 1980s. The rate of new, high-calorie bakery foods also jumped substantially. A revealing graphic of this trend, charted against the rise in obesity rates, was published by the *American Journal of Clinical Nutrition* in 1999; the two lines in remarkable tandem.

The increased variety in snacks and sweets enabled by the Butzian revolution in agriculture conjured a new and ever fattening pattern of eating. Just as the presence of supersized portions had stimulated Americans to eat more at mealtime, the *sheer presence* of a large variety of new high-calorie snacks was deeply reshaping the *overall habits* of the American eater. . . .

And snack kids did. In the 80s, in every single age group, between-meal chomping was louder than ever. Moreover, the troubling tendency to snack several times every day—in essence, making snacking part of a de facto meal pattern—was perpetuating itself into adolescence and young adulthood. . . .

---

*New studies show that, far from the romanticized "eat when you feel like it" philosophy, eating more often in itself may make one fat, regardless of the calorie count.*

---

The demographics of increased snacking also revealed a new and disturbing trend: The most avid snackers were the poor. In the same period the snacking rate per day among low-income households went from 67 percent to 82 percent. Snacking by whites increased the least while snacking by Hispanics and African Americans increased the most. The greatest increases were in the poor-to-middle-class South. And like meals in fast-food joints, the calorie density of snacks was growing. As Popkin concluded, "This large increase in total energy and energy density of snacks among young adults in the U.S. may be contributing to our obesity epidemic."

Beyond the immediate contribution of more calories to the diet, the very nature of modern snacking may be pushing children toward obesity. New studies show that, far from the romanticized "eat when you feel like it" philosophy, eating more often in itself may make one fat, regardless of the caloric count. . . .

In other words, a perpetually snacking child—whether he knows best or not—is literally a walking, talking, fat-making machine. One that knows no limits.

If the parents of the early '80s had, in essence, let the calories in, they would soon be aided in doing so by a most unlikely accomplice: the public school system.

Until the mid-'70s, public high schools were still a bastion of traditional postwar culture, a place where the boundaries, however frayed, still held. In postwar America, . . . a . . . standard-bearer of campus life concerned food. Nutritionally, the cafeteria of the '70s still reigned as the center of activity for those cool enough to have parents who didn't—or couldn't, or wouldn't—pack a lunch for them. There were Coke machines, but they were few and they dispensed a mere six to eight ounces at a time, and were peripheral to campus life, the places where amateur smokers cadged a quick one between classes.

Such, at least, were the lingering images of public schools held by many '80s parents, who were (sometimes consciously and often not) hoping that the duties they no longer had time for at home might somehow be fulfilled at school.

---

*By 1999, 95 percent of 345 California high schools surveyed by the non-profit Public Health Institute were offering branded fast foods as à la carte entree items for lunch.*

---

By the time Me Generation parents began handing their children over to the schools, though, the empire had changed. . . . The final blow to the old empire came in the form of budgetary cutbacks. . . .

In California, where famously well-funded schools had long enjoyed *primus inter pares* status, school cafeterias felt the first pinch, and the way they reacted to it foreshadowed how school lunch programs nationwide would deal with similar cuts.

In 1981 the California Department of Education ended its successful Food Service Equipment Program. For decades the program had augmented local school budgets by providing millions of dollars for the maintenance and upgrading of school cafeterias. For the Los Angeles Unified School District (LAUSD), then experiencing unprecedented growth, the cut "was a huge blow," says Laura Chinnock, now the assistant director of the district's mammoth food services department. "What that did was to force us to make changes in the existing infrastructure instead of expanding. So now we had to feed, say, two thousand kids through the old service windows that were built to service half that. Well, now double *that*—and keep in mind that the minimum legal amount of time for a child to eat lunch is twenty minutes—and you'll see why now some big schools have kids lining up at ten-thirty in the morning for lunch." . . .

---

*For a decade firms like Taco Bell and Pizza Hut had tried—with occasional success—to develop institutional feeding programs.*

---

For a decade firms like Taco Bell and Pizza Hut had tried—with occasional success—to develop institutional feeding programs. One way to do that was to sell frozen versions of their most popular products to large institutions. But frozen entrees never quite captured the imagination, let alone the taste buds, of increasingly sophisticated pizza chompers. Worse, to make the effort really work, fast-food makers would have to spend a great deal of money reformulating their products to meet

USDA limits on fats and sugars in school lunch foods. . . . There had to be a way—but where was it?

The answer came in the early 1990s, when a group of enterprising Pizza Hut salespeople asked: Why not—instead of trying to qualify Pizza Hut pizzas under the school lunch program—find a way to sell the pizzas outside of the federally regulated cafeterias, say, out on the lawn, or on the playground, or even over by the old vending machine areas? The executives took the idea to several large school districts. One of them was Los Angeles Unified. There, as one nutrition director says, "it was as if this huge light bulb went on." Not only could the district get out of the never ending battles with the USDA and Pizza Hut over re-formulation, it could also make some money on its own by purchasing the pizzas centrally and then selling them at a markup. And by offering a branded product, they might additionally keep students off the streets and on campus. . . .

---

*In the early 1990s . . . a group of enterprising Pizza Hut salespeople asked: Why not . . . sell the pizzas outside of the federally regulated cafeteria, say, out on the lawn, or on the playground?*

---

By 1999, 95 percent of 345 California high schools surveyed by the non-profit Public Health Institute were offering branded fast foods as à la carte entree items for lunch. At 71 percent of those schools, fast food made up a substantial portion of total food sales—up to 70 percent. Seventy-two percent of the same schools permitted fast-food and beverage advertising on campus.

But what really was wrought? Who really was served? Certainly anti–fast-food activists now had a genuine beef with school administration. Not only had "the system" found a way around the well-intended (and very healthy) USDA guidelines, it had also instigated another problem: dietary overconsumption. Portion sizes for pizza were a case in point. The cafeteria dispensed individual pizzas that, by law. corresponded to USDA portion recommendations. In the LAUSD, for example, a typical individual school lunch pizza runs somewhere around 5.5 ounces. A typical food cart, or branded, pizza—sold outside the cafeteria and thus unrestrained by such regulation—weighs in at almost twice that. The school lunch pizza had 375 calories, the branded "personal" pizza more than twice that—almost one-third of the recommended daily calories for a typical American teenager. The schools had lost control of calories.

# TV Marketing of Junk Food Affects Children's Food Preferences

*Sally Squires*

*Sally Squires is health and nutrition columnist for the* Washington Post. *Her "Lean Plate Club" column is widely syndicated.*

Parents who stock their kitchens with healthy food, limit eating out, and ensure that their children stay active may overlook a threat to their best efforts to keep their kids lean: the television.

As a new report from the Kaiser Family Foundation showed [in spring 2007], children and teens get bombarded with thousands of food ads yearly. So many, in fact, that they add up fifty-one hours of viewing time yearly for kids ages eight to twelve; nearly forty-one hours for those thirteen to seventeen and about thirty hours among those two to seven.

## A Wasteland of Candy and Snacks

That might not be a problem if the ads promoted nutritious fare, such as fruit, vegetables, whole grains, and low-fat dairy products. But the report—the largest ever conducted of food marketing to children and teens—highlights how TV commercials tout mostly junk food. Candy and snacks accounted for a third of the food commercials, while 28 percent were for cereals, many of them loaded with added sugar, and 10 percent were for fast food.

Lest you think that these ads might not be having much effect, consider this: A 2006 Institute of Medicine report found that food ads and marketing strongly influence children's food preferences and their diets.

## Translating Preferences into Demand

Any parent who has shopped for groceries with children probably knows firsthand the strength of this marketing effort. Science has documented that "the foods that are being advertised are the ones that children are going to be asking their parents to purchase," says Mary Story, who studies food marketing to children at the University of Minnesota in Minneapolis.

How often do parents give in to the pleas for junk food? About 50 percent of the time, according to Story's research of family members shopping for groceries together.

## International Regulation vs. U.S. Laxity

Fifty percent of countries now regulate food marketing to children, according to an editorial by New York University nutrition professor Marion Nestle published last year in the *New England Journal of Medicine*. Australia bans food advertisements aimed at children fourteen and younger. In the Netherlands, food companies can't advertise sweets to kids younger than twelve. Sweden prohibits the use of cartoon characters to promote foods to children younger than twelve.

The United States has far fewer regulations. But the Institute of Medicine report advised that Congress enact more rules "if the industry does not change its practices voluntarily."

Since then, the Ad Council and the National Advertising Review Council have launched voluntary self-regulation efforts designed to help control food marketing and promote healthier messages to younger TV viewers.

"The Institute of Medicine and members of Congress on both sides of the aisle, including Senator Sam Brownback and Senator Tom Harkin, have sent messages that they want, and expect to see, some substantial changes in food advertising to kids," said Vicky Rideout, vice president and director of Kaiser's Program for the Study of Entertainment Media and Health, who directed the latest study. "It's also very clear that they are not prepared to mandate changes until they give the industry a chance to do something voluntarily."

Some critics say that is not enough. "There is a lot of talk of companies' commitment to addressing junk-food marketing to kids," notes Margo Wootan, director of nutrition for the Center for Science in the Public Interest, a consumer advocacy group.

"But overwhelmingly the messages promote unhealthy eating. . . . We have been very patient in encouraging the industry to do the right thing. If industry is not going to self-regulate, then the courts and Congress are going to need to step in and do it."

# Schools Offering Fast Food Sacrifice Student Health for Profits

*Kelly D. Brownell and Katherine Battle Horgen*

*Kelly D. Brownell is a psychology professor at Yale University and director of the Yale Center for Eating and Weight Disorders. Katherine Battle Horgen is on the staff at the Yale Center for Eating and Weight Disorders.*

Children intersect with food in many ways in a typical school, some more obvious than others.

## Channel One and Food Advertising

Television food ads have invaded the schools. Channel One shows ten minutes of news and two minutes of ads in its daily broadcast to school-children. In return, schools get "free" video equipment. The broadcast reaches 12,000 schools, 400,000 educators, and 8 million teenage viewers, and in return for access, each school receives $25,000 in equipment. Ads cost about $175,000 for a thirty-second spot and are promoted as reaching 40 percent of American teens.

Researchers studying the impact of Channel One found that 69 percent of commercials broadcast over a four-week period were for food products, which included fast food, candy, soft drinks, and snack chips. The study found that Channel One influenced the children's thoughts about the products advertised, enhanced their consumer orientations, increased their intent to purchase the products, and led to in-

Kelly D. Brownell and Katherine Battle Horgen, "Junk Food 101: Schools, Commercialism, and Unhealthy Eating," *Food Fight: The Inside Story of the Food Industry, America's Obesity Crisis, and What We Can Do About It.* New York: McGraw-Hill, 2004, pp. 129–60. Copyright © by The McGraw-Hill Companies, Inc. All rights reserved. Reproduced by permission.

creased positive feelings about the products. The study did not, however, find that students at schools broadcasting Channel One were more likely than their peers to report buying the products.

Some argue that children are exposed to marketing anyway, so schools may as well benefit. School officials have even argued that they have more control over the type of messages delivered when commercials are shown at school, thereby protecting children.

Some parents limit their childs's exposure to advertising, but Channel One, under the guise of education, has found a way under the radar. Channel One boasts of this, saying in one ad, "Channel One delivers the hardest to reach teen viewers. Channel One even penetrates the lightest viewers among teens."

---

*The number of school hours given to Channel One cost taxpayers $1.8 billion per year; the two minutes of commercials alone cost $300 million in lost school time.*

---

Advertising to children in school may undermine what children learn in health classes, uses time that could be devoted to education, adds to the already high level of advertising to which children are exposed, and may be seen as an endorsement of the advertised products by the school. Too little research exists on the impact of in-school advertising, but the negative impact can be imagined or inferred from the amount food companies spend to advertise.

Channel One exposure sums to six hours of commercials per year and thirty-six total hours of time that could have been spent on instruction. Participation may not be voluntary. Two Ohio teens who protested the programming by walking out were sent to the local juvenile detention center.

## Challenges to Channel One's Advertising

Several states nave begun to question the impact of Channel One and have ended contracts. Parents in several states have filed lawsuits against schools airing Channel One but refusing other activities. Many of Alabama's public schools have distanced themselves from Channel One, spurred by the findings of Birmingham-based watchdog group Obligation, Inc., which provides information on the content and effects of the program.

One report estimated that the number of school hours given to Channel One costs taxpayers $1.8 billion per year; the two minutes of commercials alone cost $300 million in lost school time. Equipment rental would be cheaper. The study estimated an annual rental value of the equipment at $4,000 per school, but the value of the lost time at $158,000 per school. The study also reported that Channel One makes a $30 million annual profit.

If access to television news is important, schools could subscribe to services such as CNN Newsroom, which is commercial free and free of charge.

## Junk Food Infiltrates Educational Materials

Imagine the product exposure when young children learn their numbers by counting Tootsie Rolls, M&M's, and Skittles. One company published a math textbook for elementary school students that included the following problems:

- Pop Secret popcorn claims that only 250 of every 500 kernels meet its high standards. Write a ratio comparing numbers of good kernels to the number examined in simplest form.

- Jerry and five friends bought a six-pack of Gatorade to drink after their baseball game. Each friend wants to pay for his share of the Gatorade. If the six-pack costs $2.49, how much does each friend owe to the nearest cent?

- What is your favorite color of M&M's? What fraction of that color do you think a package would contain?

The company noted that it was not paid by the food companies, but this and other examples of the commercializing of education were criticized in the press. The book was approved for use in fifteen states.

An article in an education newsletter cited more learn-by-counting-food books, including *Skittles Math Riddles*, *Reese's Pieces: Count by Fives*, and the *Hershey Milk Chocolate Bar Fractions Book*. Some bookstores, teachers, and even publishers have chosen to reject such books and pediatricians and parents have spoken out against publicizing unhealthy food through academics.

State laws that require textbook screening do not govern the use of corporate-sponsored "educational items." The Consumers Union evaluated corporate-sponsored materials and found that 80 percent favored the company's agenda and/or included biased or incomplete information.

Product placement in classroom material is orchestrated by savvy advertising companies who recognize the buying power of a captive student audience. Lifetime Learning Systems of Fairfield, Connecticut, advertised that companies can "take your message into the classroom, where the young people you want to reach are forming attitudes that will last a lifetime." One cartoonlike ad showed kids rushing ahead with dollars in hand, the caption reading, "They're ready to spend, and we reach them."

## Food as an Academic Incentive

Incentive programs can support laudable goals like encouraging children to attend school, read, and do homework, but prizes tend to be things like donuts and pizza. . . . The most common rewards for good academic performance, behavior, and attendance are pizza, candy, and soft drinks.

Several major food companies are involved. Pizza Hut's Book It! Program, in its seventeenth year, is a well-known example of an incentive program. Students are rewarded for meeting reading goals with free pizza, and now the program includes both elementary students and preschoolers. In a Detroit elementary school, McDonald's constructed a Mini McDonald's where students could earn meals through reading, quizzes, and good school attendance. A mural of McDonald's characters was placed on the cafeteria wall.

Dunkin' Donuts has a program called "Grade A Donuts: Honoring Homework Stars." Teachers can order a kit that includes an activity guide, "Homework Heroes" booklets for children, a classroom poster, and sets of coupons, each good for two free donuts. The program aims to "reward students and their homework helpers for good homework habits."

Programs like these have both benefits and costs. We are not aware of whether these incentives improve school performance or whether food acts as a more powerful reward than alternative prizes like small toys. Drawbacks must be considered because such programs may influence food habits. Certainly other incentives could be used (movie passes, toys, etc.).

## Selling Advertising Space in Schools

Placing advertisements or company logos in prominent locations has also become part of what schools sell to soft drink companies. Score boards with company logos are common, but other forms of advertising also occur. One university in Connecticut, where swim meets are held for children of all ages, has padded deck chairs around the pool with Coca-Cola in bright red letters against a white background. A Dallas high school near the Dallas-Fort Worth airport was paid to have the Dr. Pepper logo painted on its rooftop for advertising to arriving flights.

Soft drink machines themselves are advertisements. The fronts of such machines are generally brightly colored and feature well-lit company logos, usually with pictures of the drinks. All students, no matter whether they buy the products, pass by the machines and are exposed to advertising.

---

*Providing food is often seen as a necessary service, much as custodial service might be.*

---

School buses have become moving advertisements. Although the National Association of State Directors of Pupil Transportation and the National Conference on School Transportation have encouraged banning ads for safety reasons, buses continue to be covered. The New York City Board of Education hopes to raise $53 million annually by allowing ads on the district's buses. Colorado school buses advertise 7-Up and Old Navy.

Schools and food companies think of ever more clever ways to collaborate. Joining the age-old ads in school newspapers, yearbooks, and programs for theatrical, musical, and sporting events, there are reports of advertising and corporate logos on school-sponsored television stations, recognition on a school district's voice mail system, "spirit buses" with a school's logo along with the logo from Burger King, signs in hallways, and logos on posters, calendars, book covers, and mouse pads.

## Food as Fund-Raising

The National PTA held its 2002 convention in San Antonio. The *New York Times* published an article on the meeting, discussing not education but sugar. The *Times* reported that the booths in the exhibit hall displayed software, books, testing materials, and candy. Mars, Nestle, and Hershey were among the "confectioners" who distributed free samples of candy and did their best to convince local PTAs to sell candy for fundraisers.

Another exhibitor at the meeting was the Sugar Association. They distributed brochures saying that sugar does not cause obesity or tooth decay, and added, "If your child loves sweet treats, there's no need to worry." The association says that sugar used in moderation can be part of a balanced diet.

The National PTA and school administrators realize the inconsistency of selling candy to promote education. Many must have misgivings, but ultimately yield in an attempt to support the schools. The conflict between principle and practice is shown in the following two quotes:

*National PTA supports policies that protect students from exploitation by prohibiting programs in schools that require students to view advertising.*

*—National PTA position statement on commercialization in schools*

*Shirley Igo, the National PTA President, said that when schools could not pay for their instructional programs, PTAs helped fill the gap, and that candy sales were only one way to do so.*

Two things might change the situation. Pressure and concern from both parents and teachers might make health salient enough to prevail over the need for revenue, and other ways could be developed to replace the money now generated from food sales. . . .

## Schools Do Not Consider Healthy Eating Relevant to Their Mission

What children eat has not typically been viewed as important to a school's educational mission. Providing food is often seen as a necessary service, much as custodial service might be, and is expected to generate a profit or at least break even. Ironically, earning money from selling energy-dense food is thought to promote education, as it helps buy a scoreboard, fund school trips, and so on.

---

*Schools receive only $2.14 for each free meal they serve as part of the National School Lunch Program, often not enough to break even.*

---

Food service directors get stuck in a tug-of-war. On one hand is their desire to serve healthy foods and to see children thrive. The American School Food Service Association, for instance, has excellent materials not only on school lunch programs, but on general nutrition information for children and parents.

Tugging in the opposite direction is pressure from the schools to make money. Absorbing a loss might be acceptable if needed education were occurring and the cafeteria were considered a classroom, but residing outside the educational mainstream as it does, food service must focus on income.

A different conceptual stance is to view food as one key to making a school a top-rate educational institution and to agree that creating a healthy environment supercedes the need for income. Several changes then become obvious. Considering the cafeteria a laboratory for learning, where children eat in a healthy manner but also learn about nutrition, would be one move forward. Integrating nutrition education with both health education and physical education could generate consistent, powerful messages about the importance of good diet. The most important step of all, however, is to get better control over foods available in school. Schools making such conceptual and structural changes would stand out and would probably benefit from public reaction.

## Popular Foods Bring in More Money

As long as schools need the extra money and selling popular food provides it, there are heavy incentives for schools to continue current practices. Schools receive only $2.14 for each free meal they serve as part of the National School Lunch Program, often not enough to break even, while the profit margins on à la carte foods and items sold in vending machines can be 50 percent to 100 percent. An example from a *Time* magazine article entitled "Flunking Lunch" is Northside Independent School District in San Antonio. The cost for an entire federal lunch is $1.75, while students pay $2 for just one slice of Papa John's pizza, which is more than double what the schools pay to buy it. . . .

## If Unhealthy Foods Are Available, Children Will Eat Them

It is clear from research with both humans and laboratory animals that providing access to foods high in sugar, fat, and calories leads to overeating. Introducing healthier options into the picture does not have an appreciable effect on the appeal or consumption of the high-fat, high-sugar foods.

One study found that 76 percent of schools sell pizza, burgers, or sandwiches; 80 percent have high-fat cakes and cookies; and 62 percent sell French fries as à la carte items. But in addition, 90 percent have fruits and vegetables and 48 percent sell low-fat yogurt or low-fat cookies or pastry. Still, the diet is in dire condition. For most children, for most of the time, healthy foods will be eaten if only healthy foods are available and if unhealthy foods are not available as competition.

The implication? Schools should not have unhealthy foods, at any time, at any place, in any amounts. Having healthier items added to a menu containing unhealthy favorites will help a few children, but most will go for the favorites. . . .

# Banning Fast-Food Advertising Would Not Reduce Childhood Obesity

*Radley Balko*

*Radley Balko previously worked as a policy analyst for the libertarian Cato Institute, specializing in vice and civil liberties issues. He is a columnist for* FoxNews.com, *a senior editor for* Reason *magazine, and has been widely published. He keeps a libertarian blog (TheAgitator.com) and lives outside of Washington, D.C.*

Should manufacturers of so-called "low-nutrition" foods be allowed to market their products to children? The answer, according to many food scolds, is no.

The Institute of Medicine—a private group with funding from the Center[s] for Disease Control—held hearings in Washington, D.C., recently to ask various food industry executives why they are marketing harmful products to children. This came on the heels of a media blitz by the lofty-sounding Center for Science in the Public Interest (CSPI), which issued a plan calling for restrictions of junk food, including a complete ban on cross-promotional campaigns—think SpongeBob SquarePants Cereal.

"Ideally," the CSPI press release proclaimed, "only healthful foods like fruits, vegetables, and whole-grain products would be marketed to kids."

Even if we set free speech concerns to the side, ad bans make for bad public policy for a number of reasons.

## Why Bans Don't Work

*Ad bans have failed everywhere they've been tried.* The list so far includes Sweden, Quebec, and Norway. None of these

Radley Balko, "Don't Blame SpongeBob for Childhood Obesity," *Cato Institute*, March 2, 2005, www.cato.org/pub_display.php?pub_id=3696. Reproduced by permission.

places have shown significant reductions in child obesity. In Sweden, the restrictions have been in place for a decade, yet the country's childhood obesity rates are in line with the rest of Europe.

*There's no correlation between ad exposure and childhood obesity.* George Mason University's Todd Zywicki noted at a forum last summer that the average American child actually watches *less* TV than he did 15 years ago. What's more, children face less exposure to food ads now than they did then, for a variety of reasons. The remote control has made ad-watching optional over the last 20 years, and more recent technology like TiVo may make traditional commercials completely obsolete.

Broadcast television is also losing younger viewers to cable, where ads in general are 40 percent less prevalent and where food ads comprise about half the percentage of overall ad time that they do in broadcast. Cable also offers more options for channel-flipping during commercials, and premium cable stations like HBO, which have no commercials at all, have become popular. All told, the average American child viewed 900 *fewer* food commercials in 2003 than he did in 1994. That this same average child *gained* weight amounts to a pretty solid rebuttal to the theory that food marketing is a significant contributor to childhood obesity.

*You'd need to ban ads in adult programming.* The fact is, you simply can't limit a kid's exposure to food ads, unless you're prepared to ban *all* food advertising. Most children's television viewing isn't limited to children's television programming. Kids watch shows intended for adults, too.

In fact, the kids most prone to obesity—those with minimal parental supervision—are also very likely most likely to watch adult programming. Former Federal Trade Commission administrator Timothy Muris pointed out in a conference last June that if Congress had caved and banned food ads aimed at kids the first time the idea was proposed in the 1970s, the only television show that would have been affected would have been *Captain Kangaroo.*

---

*Holding Tony the Tiger, the Nabisco elves, or SpongeBob responsible for childhood obesity is certainly the easiest public policy prescription.*

---

Today, such a ban would probably hit a few other programs as well, which brings us to the next point . . . [sic]

*The ban would cripple children's television.* The FCC [Federal Communication Commission] already mandates that broadcasters devote a portion of the broadcast day to children's programming. Food ads make up a huge portion of the ad revenue for those programs. Cut off that ad revenue, and the broadcasters subject to FCC regulation lose any incentive to invest in high-quality children's television. Why put money into a sure loser?

Furthermore, television not subject to FCC regulations—cable, for example—would likely drastically cut back on the amount of television time it carves out for children, or just disregard children's programming entirely.

## Obesity Is a More Complex Issue than Fast Food

*The cause of childhood obesity lies elsewhere.* Several recent studies have suggested that the single best indicator of a child's health, diet, weight, and activity level is the health, diet, weight, and activity level of that child's parents. Children of active parents tend to be active. Kids tend to eat what their moms and dads eat.

That said, there's also some evidence that the caloric intake among kids hasn't changed much over the last quarter century. What *has* changed is the amount of time kids are active, outside, and exercising. Kids today may watch less television, but they more than make up for it with video games, Internet activity, DVDs, or some combination of the three.

Holding Tony the Tiger, the Nabisco elves, or SpongeBob responsible for childhood obesity is certainly the easiest public policy prescription for childhood obesity. It would be much more difficult, and perilous, to charge parents with neglect or child abuse for allowing their kids to get dangerously fat.

But ultimately a child's diet and exercise habits *do* begin with his parents. The food industry can't be faulted for putting products on the shelves that sell, nor can it be faulted for marketing those products to the people who will pester their parents to buy them.

# Inactivity, Not Soft Drinks, Is to Blame for Obesity

*Richard Berman*

*Richard Berman is the executive director of the Center for Consumer Freedom, an advocacy group of restaurants, food industry corporations, and individual consumers.*

When it comes to childhood obesity, the raging debate over soda being sold in schools has about as much substance as the time-worn question: How many angels can dance on the head of a pin?

According to a 2002 study, the average kid gets one half of 1 percent of his or her calories from vending machines. While that is admittedly up from one third of 1 percent in the 1970s, it seems that limiting vending machines to water won't make a big difference.

And the more political energy expended on vending machines, the less there will be left to address the real cause of childhood obesity: physical inactivity.

## Inactivity Leads to Obesity

Former Food and Drug Administration commissioner Mark McClellan observes, "Actual levels of caloric intake among the young haven't appreciably changed over the last 20 years."

Study after study corroborates McClellan's point.

A study published in the *Journal of Clinical Endocrinology & Metabolism* pointed out: "It is often assumed that the increase in pediatric obesity has occurred because of an increase in caloric intake. However, the data do not substantiate this."

Translation: The problem won't be found in vending machines. It's in the gym. It's in the recess yard. And it's in our

Richard Berman, "Soft Drinks in Schools Aren't to Blame for Obese Children," *Center for Consumer Freedom*, August 18, 2005. www.consumerfreedom.com/oped_detail.cfm/oped/337. Reproduced by permission.

neighborhoods, where kids now spend far, far more time with their Xboxes than they do running around outside or biking with friends.

Walking and biking trips by children have dropped more than 60 percent since the late 1970s. A full quarter of American children get no physical activity whatsoever.

---

*Does any rational person think that replacing a zero-calorie beverage with milk or juice will . . . prevent weight gain?*

---

## Public-Interest Groups Manipulate Data

So why are we so quick to blame vending machines? Public attitudes have been skillfully manipulated by interest groups, whose greatest concern is that someone, somewhere may be enjoying what they eat and drink.

Anti-soda activists—who also seek extra taxes and warning labels on soft drinks, as well as tobacco-style class-action lawsuits—have an insatiable thirst for regulating our diets. They allege soda makers' new school distribution policy doesn't go far enough. They want a complete ban on soda in all schools.

In other words, a young man or woman old enough to carry a gun in Iraq won't always be able to choose his or her own beverage.

America's dedicated diet scolds also want diet soda out of schools. Pop may have unfairly drawn the short stick in the obesity blame game. But does any rational person think that replacing a zero-calorie beverage with milk or juice will do anything to prevent weight gain?

# Environmental Factors and Genetics Are the Source of Obesity

*Barry Glassner*

*Barry Glassner is a professor of sociology at the University of Southern California and the author of* The Culture of Fear.

The list of explanations for what got us fat over the past quarter century, each with its own ring of truth and band of devoted scientists, activists, and dieters, is longer than a well-stocked smorgasbord. Journalists and government officials typically favor what I call the "fiscal model," which holds that "energy is deposited by eating food, that exercise and metabolism withdraw it, and that body fat is a sort of corporeal balance sheet," as S. Bryn Austin, an instructor at the Harvard School of Medicine and critic of the model, summarized. A version of the gospel of naught, the fiscal model blames the obesity epidemic on overeating and inactivity. As a writer for *U.S. News & World Report* put it, "Over-weight results from one thing: eating more food than one burns in physical activity."

Believers in the fiscal model contend that in the absence of additional exercise, it took no more than a few extra bites or slurps a day by most Americans to produce the obesity epidemic. "To gain 15 pounds in a year, you only have to have an imbalance of 150 calories a day, which is one soft drink," Dr. Thomas Robinson, an obesity researcher at Stanford, told a *New York Times* reporter. "Even a Life Saver is 10 calories. An extra Life Saver a day is a pound a year."

In this view, calories are like germs. Proponents of the fiscal model speak of calories lurking in unexpected places and finding their way into our bodies when we're scarcely aware. The notion dates back to 1918, when Lulu Hunt Peters published *Diet and Health with Key to the Calories*, America's first diet bestseller. The book brought the concept of the calorie to the general public. "You should know and also use the word calorie as frequently, or more frequently, than you use the words foot, yard, quart, gallon, and so forth," Peters instructed. "Hereafter you are going to eat calories of food. Instead of saying one slice of bread, or a piece of pie, you will say 100 calories of bread, 350 calories of pie."

---

*The obesity epidemic materialized over a couple of decades, whereas genes take at least a couple of generations to change.*

---

Generations of Americans have followed her command, aided, during much of the period when our collective weight shot up, by federally mandated labeling of the calorie content of every packaged food product. . . .

## A Red Herring

Some argue it is the types of foods Americans eat that have made us fat. "Fat makes you fat," the diet guru of the 1990s, Susan Powter, famously proclaimed, and Dr. Dean Ornish, of *Eat More, Weigh Less* fame, continues to preach that gospel. Other diet docs, carrying forward the teachings of the late Robert Atkins, insist it's the carbohydrates. And some, like the South Beach Diet mogul Arthur Agatston, split the difference. Rather than excommunicate either food group entirely, they banish only those they deem "bad fats" and "bad carbs."

Or maybe the emphasis on food is itself misguided. "There is no evidence that fat people consistently eat more than the lean," William Bennett, a Harvard Medical School physician and longtime editor of the *Harvard Medical School Health Letter*, reported in 1982. In a book he cowrote that year with Joel Gurin, editor of *American Health* magazine, and in articles in medical journals over the next dozen years, Bennett showed that you cannot predict people's weight gain by how much they eat.

"Food is a red herring," he wrote. "It is perfectly possible for some people to eat a lot and gain very little, whereas others gain weight while eating abstemiously." Armed with experiments showing that fat people consume no more calories than thin people, Bennett described the fiscal model as fatally flawed—a conclusion supported by later studies that compared the diets of men and women across a wide weight range, and by studies of twins. In these latter experiments, scientists fed pairs of identical twins many more calories than they customarily ate or, conversely, put them on an exercise regimen to "burn off" calories. After a few weeks, there was great variation *between* the pairs of twins but hardly any *within* each pair. Unrelated individuals gained or lost widely different amounts, while differences between twin siblings were minimal. This implies that people's weight is governed more by their genes than by how many calories they eat or deplete.

---

*The obesity rate increased by a whopping 30 percent between 1991 and 2001 . . . the typical American gained less than a pound a year.*

---

Those who prefer to blame the obesity epidemic on food and sloth consider it absurd to propose that genes may be an important culprit. The obesity epidemic materialized over a couple of decades, whereas genes take at least a couple of *generations* to change, they correctly note, and from those facts, they wrongly infer that the epidemic must have resulted from America's "food-rich, activity-poor environment" and "a certain sin known as gluttony, which has somehow gotten a good name," as author Greg Critser says in his book, *Fat Land: How Americans Became the Fattest People in the World* (2003).

To the extent that devotees of the fiscal model grant any role to inheritance, they favor the so-called thrifty gene hypothesis. Because our ancestors frequently faced food shortages and famine, that story goes, we evolved to eat and store energy. In an environment of easy access to cheap and appetizing calories, we're programmed to gobble up and retain more than we need. The real surprise is that anyone stays thin in such an environment.

Twin studies and actual patterns of obesity in the United States tell a different tale. There seems to be no species-wide tendency; rather, only a relatively small minority of people appear to be disposed to obesity. Jeffrey Friedman, a prominent obesity researcher at Rockefeller University, has shown that the obesity rate shot up not as a result of big increases in weight throughout the population, but rather because of a threshold effect. A sufficient number of Americans were just below the cutoff for what officially qualifies as obese. By gaining a modest amount of weight, they crossed the threshold and got reclassified from "overweight" to "obese." Although the obesity rate increased by a whopping 30 percent between 1991 and 2001, for example, the typical American gained less than a pound a year. But that fairly modest weight gain was enough to push substantial numbers over the threshold from "overweight" to "obese."

Friedman notes that many Americans added little or no weight during the obesity epidemic. Only the very obese added twenty-five pounds or more, and different ethnic groups gained different amounts of weight. These facts strongly suggest, Friedman argues, that a subgroup within the population is genetically predisposed to obesity and another subgroup is not. The two subgroups may have different genetic lineages, he contends. The portion of the U.S. population whose ancestors resided in the Fertile Crescent and parts of Europe where a favorable climate or domestication of plants and animals made food shortages less of a problem may actually have inherited a *resistance* to obesity. "Might it be," Friedman asks, "that it is the obese who carry the 'hunter-gatherer' genes and the lean that carry the 'Fertile Crescent' or 'Western' genes?"

The principal point of natural selection is to ensure reproduction, after all, and obesity increases the likelihood of miscarriage. So as Friedman suggests, "where the risk of starvation is reduced, one might expect genes that resist obesity and its complications to have a selective advantage."

## The Law of Unintended Consequences

Or maybe neither bad genes nor Big Macs are the right place to look for the causes of the obesity epidemic. Another large body of evidence points in a different direction, to changes in the American economy. During the decades when Americans' weight shot up, so did levels of economic hardship and insecurity. In the 1980s and 1990s, more Americans lost their jobs than at any time since the Great Depression, and those who did have jobs worked longer hours. About a third of the population became poorer during this period, and millions more had difficulties maintaining their lifestyles because the raises they received did not keep up with inflation.

Who suffered the most from these misfortunes? The same sectors of the population who gained the most weight: low-income Americans and ethnic minorities. The wealthiest 20 percent of Americans—who now control about 80 percent of the nation's total wealth—have relatively low rates of obesity. So do those whose socioeconomic status has improved.

A key link between the obesity epidemic and economic hardship is chronic stress. Stress provokes the body to produce less growth hormone, a substance that reduces fat deposits and speeds up metabolism, and *more* of what are called stress hormones, which provoke cravings for soothing substances like glazed doughnuts and chocolate fudge ice cream.

People don't invariably respond to stress by gobbling comfort foods, however. Many opt instead for cigarettes, and therein lies a luscious little irony. The obesity epidemic that government agencies and advocacy groups are battling to reverse resulted in part from the success of antismoking campaigns by these same organizations in the recent past. The number of smokers declined by about a third during the 1980s and 1990s, and when people give up smoking, they tend to gain weight.

---

*A Frappuccino is as oversized and calorie-laden as anything McDonald's can dream up.*

---

We social scientists call this the law of unintended consequences. Roughly the sociological equivalent of Newton's third law, it holds that any social intervention that produces beneficial outcomes will be likely to give rise to unintended negative effects as well. The obesity epidemic cannot be explained entirely, though, by way of the law of unintended consequences. Even a valid application of the law, such as the connection between antismoking campaigns and obesity, accounts for only a fraction of the nation's added tonnage. (The ranks of the obese include people who never smoked, and some people give up smoking without getting fat.) . . .

## Why Fast Food Takes the Fall

Anyone who dislikes fast food can go after that industry. According to a standard explanation for both the obesity epidemic and its concentration among the lower classes, "America's least well-off are so surrounded by double cheeseburgers, chicken buckets, extra-large pizzas, and supersized fries that they are more likely to be overweight than the population as a whole" (Gregg Easterbrook in the *New York Times*).

Even putting aside the broader failings of the fiscal model from which it is derived, and the problems of chronology I mentioned at the outset, the fast-food theory has little to commend it. As a prominent obesity researcher at the U.S. Department of Health and Human Services who asked to remain anonymous told me, "There's a lot of subtle and not so subtle bias. From going to all these talks about the obesity epidemic, you would think that McDonald's and other places where the 'wrong' sort of lower-class people eat are calorie-dripping hellholes, and expensive classy restaurants serve only fat-free vegetables and no desserts.

"No one ever uses Starbucks as an example, but a Frappuccino is as oversized and calorie-laden as anything McDonald's can dream up. But the person giving the talk probably goes to Starbucks him- or herself and wouldn't be caught dead at McDonald's."

---

*Teens from families that eat together consume fast food about as often as those from households that seldom have meals together . . . contrary to popular belief.*

---

Only a small number of studies have attempted to test the fast-food hypothesis directly, and they have come up with mixed results. Contrary to the impression given by some journalists and activists that dining in a fast-food restaurant "is like sitting in a room set up by aliens from another planet to fatten us up before they eat us" (Gersh Kuntzman in *Newsweek*), some studies find no association between people's body weight and whether they eat in fast-food restaurants.

What's more, some of the studies cited by advocates of the fast-food theory do not actually support it. Take this assertion from a paper in the *Journal of the American Medical Association* in 2004: "The increase in fast food consumption parallels the escalating obesity epidemic, raising the possibility that these two trends are causally related." When I dug up the only evidence the authors cite in support of that dubious claim—a paper published two years earlier—I discovered that it said no such thing. (Concerned that I had somehow missed something, I e-mailed one of the authors of the cited paper. "You're right about our article. We don't say anything about fast-food consumption," she replied.)

Or take the study of nearly five thousand adolescents that Greg Critser relies upon in *Fat Land* to support his condemnation of fast food as a perpetrator of obesity. Critser uses words like "striking" and "amazing" to describe what he saw as the study's findings, but when I read the study itself, I found something more striking than the finding Critser cites. The researchers did report, as Critser highlights, that adolescent boys who eat fast food consume more calories than boys who never visit fast-food places. And they speculated that adolescents who develop a fondness for fast food may be at greater risk of obesity later in life. But the findings of their study do not show that fast food causes obesity. Quite the opposite. "In the present study, no association was observed between frequent fast food restaurant use and obesity, even though fast food restaurant use was significantly positively associated with energy and fat intake," write the University of Minnesota epidemiologists in the *International Journal of Obesity*.

Far from finding that teens who eat fast food are fatter, they determined that boys who dine on fast food three or more times a week weigh significantly *less* than those who eat there less frequently. And teens from families that eat together consume fast food about as often as those from households that seldom have meals together, the Minnesota researchers found, contrary to popular belief.

CHAPTER 4

# Are Organic Foods a Positive Trend?

# Identifying Organic Food

*National Organic Program, Agricultural Marketing Service, United States Department of Agriculture,*

*The United States Department of Agriculture Marketing Service manages and employs programs for six industries—cotton, dairy, fruit and vegetable, livestock and seed, poultry and tobacco.*

The U.S. Department of Agriculture [USDA] has put in place a set of national standards that food labeled "organic" must meet, whether it is grown in the United States or imported from other countries. After October 21, 2002, when you buy food labeled "organic," you can be sure that it was produced using the highest organic production and handling standards in the world.

## What Is Organic Food?

Organic food is produced by farmers who emphasize the use of renewable resources and the conservation of soil and water to enhance environmental quality for future generations. Organic meat, poultry, eggs, and dairy products come from animals that are given no antibiotics or growth hormones. Organic food is produced without using most conventional pesticides; fertilizers made with synthetic ingredients or sewage sludge; bioengineering; or ionizing radiation. Before a product can be labeled "organic," a Government-approved certifier inspects the farm where the food is grown to make sure the farmer is following all the rules necessary to meet USDA organic standards. Companies that handle or process organic food before it gets to your local supermarket or restaurant must be certified, too.

USDA makes no claims that organically produced food is safer or more nutritious than conventionally produced food.

National Organic Program, "Organic Food Standards and Labels: The Facts," The Agricultural Marketing Service, United States Department of Agriculture, January 2007. http://www.ams.usda.gov/nop/consumers/brochure.html.

Organic food differs from conventionally produced food in the way it is grown, handled, and processed.

You must look at package labels and watch for signs in the supermarket [to know if food is produced organically]. Along with the national organic standards, USDA developed strict labeling rules to help consumers know the exact organic content of the food they buy. The *USDA Organic* seal also tells you that a product is at least 95 percent organic.

## Organic Food Labeling

*For single-ingredient foods*, look for the word "organic" and a small sticker version of the *USDA Organic* seal on vegetables or pieces of fruit. Or they may appear on the sign above the organic produce display.

The word "organic" and the seal may also appear on packages of meat, cartons of milk, or eggs, cheese, and other single-ingredient foods.

*For foods with more than one ingredient*, [illustrates] . . . products with less than 70 percent organic ingredients may list specific organically produced ingredients on the side panel of the package, but may not make any organic claims on the front of the package. Look for the name and address of the Government-approved certifier on all packaged products that contain at least 70 percent organic ingredients. . . .

The use of the seal is voluntary [which means that not all 100 percent organic products or products with at least 95 percent organic agreements will carry the *USDA Organic* seal].

People who sell or label a product "organic" when they know it does not meet USDA standards can be fined up to $11,000 for each violation.

## Natural Versus Organic Labels

*Natural* and *organic* are not interchangeable. Other truthful claims, such as free-range, hormone-free, and natural, can still appear on food labels. However, don't confuse these terms with "organic." Only food labeled "organic" has been certified as meeting USDA organic standards.

# Organically Produced Food Improves Human, Animal, and Environmental Health

## Peter Singer and Jim Mason

*Peter Singer is a professor of bioethics at Princeton University's Center for Human Values and the author of* Animal Liberation *(1975). Jim Mason is the author of* An Unnatural Order: Why We Are Destroying the Planet and Each Other *(1993).*

People buying organic food want to avoid unnecessary risks, and they believe that more natural methods of producing food are likely to be healthier. That belief received powerful reinforcement from the outbreak of mad cow disease in Europe and the consequent revelation that intensively farmed cattle are fed slaughterhouse remnants. From eating the meat of these cattle, at least 150 people—and some say many more—contracted a slow-acting, fatal disease. No wonder millions of consumers decided that the old ways might be safer, especially where their children are concerned. In Britain, organic baby food now accounts for half of all the baby food sold, while the German baby food market has been described as "on its way to becoming more or less exclusively organic."

Organic food contains fewer pesticides. Drawing on data covering 94,000 food samples, a Consumers Union research team found 73 percent of conventionally grown foods and 90 percent of conventionally grown apples, peaches, pears, strawberries, and celery had pesticide residues, as compared with only 23 percent of organically grown samples. Where the same pesticide was found in both conventional and organic foods, the levels of the pesticide were significantly lower in the organic food. Scientists at the University of Washington tested the urine of children eating a conventional diet and children eating predominantly organic produce and found that these differences in pesticide levels are detectable in our bodies. Some of the children on a conventional diet had pesticide byproducts in their urine that indicated an intake of pesticides above the "negligible risk" level recommended by the Environmental Protection Agency's guidelines. The children who ate organic foods had a median level of pesticide byproducts only one-sixth that of children eating conventionally farmed foods, suggesting that their intake of pesticides was well within EPA recommended limits.

---

*Children who ate organic foods had a median level of pesticide byproducts only one-sixth that of children eating conventionally farmed foods.*

---

Yet the British, French, and Swedish government food agencies have all recently concluded that there is no scientific evidence that organic food is safer or more nutritious than conventionally produced food. Michael Pollan, who has written for the *New York Times* on farming, writes: "The science might still be sketchy, but common sense tells me organic is better food—better, anyway, than the kind grown with organophosphates, with antibiotics and growth hormones, with cadmium and lead and arsenic (the EPA permits the use of toxic waste in fertilizers), with sewage sludge and animal feed made from ground-up bits of other animals as well as their own manure." . . .

## The Environment

*Organic farming maintains the quality of the soil*

When a virgin field is tilled and then fertilized with synthetic fertilizers, it will lose between 50 and 65 percent of its nitrogen and soil carbon over fifty years. After that, increasing inputs of fertilizer—and thus of fossil fuel energy—will be needed to maintain yields. If that no longer pays, the land will be abandoned, becoming a wasteland on which little grows.

Organic farming has a different philosophy. It sees farmers as stewards of the land, harvesting its fruits while they care for it so that they can leave it to future generations in a condition as good as, or better than, it was when they started farming. So organic farmers maintain and enrich the soil by adding organic matter. That increases the number of worms and micro-organisms. Soil rich in organic matter needs less irrigation because the soil holds moisture better. It is also less likely to blow away in the wind, or wash off with every storm. A study of two adjacent wheat farms on similar soil near Spokane, Washington, found that over a 37-year period, the conventional farm lost more than 8 inches of topsoil, while the organic farm lost only 2 inches. The scientists concluded that the productivity of the organic farm was being maintained, while that of the conventional farm was being reduced because of high rates of soil erosion.

---

*Organic farming . . . sees farmers as stewards of the land, harvesting its fruits while they care for it.*

---

*Organic farming fosters biodiversity*

The expansion of intensive modern agriculture, with its monoculture crops and intense use of pesticides and herbicides, threatens endangered species. Rare plants are indiscriminately sprayed with herbicides, along with more common weeds. Insecticides eliminate the prey of many birds, and small mammals may be poisoned too. Organic farms, in contrast, use no herbicides, fewer pesticides, have more organic matter in the soil, and tolerate hedges or other uncultivated areas. All this makes them a haven for endangered species of plants, insects, birds, and animals. In a survey of the evidence published in the journal *Biological Conservation* in 2005, scientists reviewed seventy-six percent separate studies comparing the impact of organic and conventional farms on such things as plants, soil microbes, earthworms, spiders, butterflies, beetles, birds, and mammals. They found that the majority of these studies demonstrated that the abundance and richness of species tends to be higher on organic farms. Significantly, the differences applied particularly to species that have experienced a decline because of the intensification of modern agriculture. In 2005, a five-year, government-funded study of British organic farms gave further support to that conclusion.

*Organic farming reduces pollution from nitrogen runoff*

Conventional agriculture relies heavily on synthetic fertilizers, especially nitrogen. World-wide, the use of nitrogen as a fertilizer has increased tenfold in the last fifty years. Half to two-thirds of this nitrogen makes its way into rivers and other ecosystems, affecting both freshwater and marine environments. The most dramatic result is the dead zone in the Gulf of Mexico. Like the dead zone in Chesapeake Bay . . . the Gulf of Mexico dead zone is caused by too much nitrogen, but here the dominant source—56 percent, according to the U.S. Geological Survey—is chemical fertilizer runoff rather than animal manure, which contributes 25 percent. The Gulf of Mexico dead zone has grown dramatically over the past twenty years, and when it peaks each summer, it now covers an area larger than the state of New Jersey. The peak comes a month after the spring use of nitrogen fertilizers in the Midwest Corn Belt—a month is the time it takes for the water from the Upper Mississippi to reach the Gulf. The expanding dead zone is disrupting fishing. This is only one of 146 dead zones around the world, and not even the largest—that is in the Baltic Sea. Nitrogen fertilizer runoff is largely responsible for most of these. Forty-three of the dead zones occur in U.S. coastal waters. A shift to organic farming, which does not use synthetic fertilizers, would dramatically reduce water pollution from nitrogen, and so shrink the dead zones.

---

*World-wide, the use of nitrogen as a fertilizer has increased tenfold in the last fifty years. Half to two-thirds . . . makes its way into rivers and other ecosystems.*

---

*Organic farming avoids the heavy pesticide and herbicide use typical of conventional farming*

Conventional farming relies heavily on pesticides, including insecticides and herbicides. Pesticide use per acre more than doubled between 1931 and 1997, although it has decreased slightly since then. . . .

Organic farmers are permitted to use only a very limited range of insecticides, selected because they are natural products or their safety is well-established. Hence, organic farms will not, to the same extent as conventional farms, release insecticides into the air or nearby rivers. They are not permitted to use any herbicides at all.

*Organic farming uses less energy for a given yield than conventional farming*

Organic farms do not use synthetic fertilizers, the manufacture of which requires a lot of energy. According to a study funded by the British Department for Environment, Food, and Rural Affairs, organic crops used 35 percent less energy per unit of production and organic dairying 74 percent less. Scientists at the University of Essex found that organic farmers in a range of different countries required only 30 to 50 percent of the energy consumed in conventional farming systems.

*Organic farming stores more carbon in the soil, thus off-setting carbon dioxide emissions*

Organic farming increases the amount of organic matter in the soil—matter that would otherwise rot above ground and produce carbon that would go into the atmosphere. So if organic farming spreads, that might reduce the severity of climate change. But how great an advantage organic farming has over conventional farming here is controversial. The Rodale Institute has carried out a 23-year study of the amount of carbon stored in the soil of its model farm and calculated that if the organic methods it uses were applied on all the cropland in the United States, 580 billion pounds of excess carbon dioxide could be sequestered in the soil every year. That's about four times the quantity of emissions that would be saved if the fuel efficiency of all cars and light trucks on U.S. roads were doubled. But questions can be raised about how long annual carbon savings could continue, since eventually the organic matter will decompose and release carbon back into the atmosphere.

---

*If the organic methods ... were applied on all the cropland in the United States, 580 billion pounds of excess carbon dioxide could be sequestered in the soil every year.*

---

In any case, much depends on what forms of organic and conventional farming are compared. Organic farmers who use a lot of compost and animal manure and periodically grow cover crops and plow them into the soil will have much more carbon in the soil than farmers who use only synthetic fertilizers and till their soil, because tilling leads to a reduction in organic matter. But the rules for being certified "organic" in the United States do not require compost, manure, or cover crops. They simply make the use of such techniques more likely by banning most other methods of keeping the soil fertile. The ideal organic farmer who practices the methods used by the Rodale Institute is making a significant contribution to reducing the carbon build-up in the atmosphere, and the standard conventional farmer is not. Buying food labeled "organic," however, does not guarantee that it was grown in keeping with the Rodale Institute methods.

There are two offsetting factors relative to climate change and organic farming to consider. It is often claimed that conventional farming produces higher yields per acre, on average, than organic farming. Therefore, if we need to produce a given quantity of food, we might use less land to produce it if we use conventional methods. Suppose we then took this extra land and planted it with trees, as part of an agro-forestry project. According to some estimates, trees absorb about eight times as much carbon per acre as soil can, even organically cultivated soil. That suggests an alternative strategy for storing carbon: grow the food we need by conventional methods on fewer acres, and plant trees on the rest. Of course, this presupposes that conventional farming really does produce higher yields than organic methods. The Rodale Institute conducted a 22-year comparative trial of conventional farming and organic farming. Although the yields from conventional farming were higher in the short-term, over the entire period of the trial, corn and soybean yields were just as high on fields farmed organically.

# Organic Foods Are Healthier for Children

*Sandra Steingraber*

*Sandra Steingraber is an ecologist and the author of* Living Downstream: An Ecologist Looks at Cancer and the Environment *(1997) and* Having Faith: An Ecologist's Journey to Motherhood *(2001).*

Organophosphate insecticides kill by attacking the nervous systems of insect pests. They are frequently used in fruit and vegetable farming. A 2003 study measured levels of these chemicals in the urine of pre-school children living in Seattle. Children with conventional diets had, on average, nine times more organophosphate insecticides in their urine than children fed organic produce. So, are organic foods healthier for our kids? Here is where science yields to mother wisdom. We in the scientific community do not yet know what levels of pesticide exposure are sufficient to endanger the health of human adults, and we know even less about their effects on children. Thus, the wide gray area called "uncertain risk."

The reasons for our ignorance are many. When researching my book, *Living Downstream:* [*An Ecologist Looks at Cancer and the Environment* (1997)] I discovered that many pesticides on the market have never been adequately screened for their ability to cause cancer. Even less thoroughly have we tested their ability to affect fetal brain growth, contribute to miscarriages, disrupt hormonal signaling, alter the onset of puberty, or undermine fertility. Evidence from animal studies suggests we have reason to be concerned about these possibilities and investigate them further.

I also learned that most human dietary studies of pesticide exposure presume adult eating habits. And yet, as any mother

Sandra Steingraber, "The Organic Manifesto of a Biologist Mother," *Organic Valley Family of Farms*, 2003. Reprinted courtesy of Organic Valley Family of Farms.

will testify, children dine on fewer foods in proportionally higher quantities than their parents do. (I do not routinely consume two bananas and two avocados a day. My twenty-seven-pound son does.) Finally, consider that young children lack many of the biological defenses that protect adults, against the toxic effects of pesticides. All of us grown-ups, for example, possess a blood-brain barrier. It works quite well to keep neurological poisons from entering the gray matter of our brains. However, we did not acquire this cerebral suit of armor until we reached the age of six months. Infants are thus far more susceptible to the brain-addling potential of insecticides and at much lower doses.

---

*If a mother's body is contaminated, so too is the child who inhabits it.*

---

Pesticides, by design, are poisons. The science shows us that most organic produce is free from pesticide residues and most conventionally grown produce is not. The science shows that children fed organic produce have significantly lower pesticide residues in their bodies than children fed conventional produce. Whatever we do or don't know about threshold levels for harm, my intuition tells me that food with no poison is better for my children's developing minds and bodies than food with some.

## Organic Foods Are Part of Good Prenatal Care

Women's bodies are the first environment. So says native American midwife Katsi Cook. This simple truth became the starting point of my book *Having Faith* [*An Ecologist's Journey to Motherhood* (2001)], which explores the intimate ecology of pregnancy. It was a project that I began during the first month of my pregnancy with the real-life Faith and finally finished a week before I gave birth to her younger brother. Those four years of research and writing can really be summed up in two simple sentences: If the world's environment is contaminated, so too is the ecosystem of a mother's body. If a mother's body is contaminated, so too is the child who inhabits it.

The placenta, which does such an admirable job at keeping bacteria and viruses out of the womb's watery habitat, is ill-equipped to serve as a barrier to toxic chemicals. Pesticides that are made up of smaller molecules are afforded free passage. They slip easily from the mother's bloodstream into the blood of the baby's umbilical cord. Pesticides made of bigger, heavier molecules are partly broken down by the placenta's enzymes before they pass through. But, ironically, this transformation sometimes renders them even *more* toxic.

We have much to learn about the reproductive effects of pesticides in use today. In the meantime, organic [food]—like sobriety, seatbelts, and not smoking—makes good prenatal sense. . . .

# Organic Production Wastes Land That Could Be Used for Direct Food Production

*Alex A. Avery*

*Alex A. Avery is director of research at the Hudson Institute's Center for Global Food Issues. The Hudson Institute is a non-partisan public policy research organization.*

The Hudson Institute's Center for Global Food Issues, an agriculture policy research group, has become identified as the leading critic of organic farming, so reporters often call us for negative quotes when they're doing a story on organic foods. The most recent example is *Newsweek*, which just ran a cover story on organic farming in time for the rollout in late October of the U.S. Department of Agriculture's new federal organic food standards.

Like so many others before them, however, the *Newsweek* reporters completely ignored our most substantive criticism.

The only quote they used—and we were the sole critics quoted—was that *E. coli* [harmful *E. coli* bacteria can cause severe discomfort and death] is "perhaps the deadliest risk in our modern food supply, and its primary hiding place is the cattle manure with which organic farmers fertilize food crops." The *Newsweek* reporters brushed this off with, "So wash your produce, but don't let it scare you."

But as we told the *Newsweek* reporters, the biggest problem with organic farming isn't food safety; it's fertilizer—actually, the lack of it.

## Organic Takes Land Out of Production

The first precept of organic farming is the decision not to use "synthetic" nitrogen fertilizer. Only "organic" nitrogen can be

Alex A. Avery, "Is the 'Organic Ethic' Ethical?" *Hudson Institute*, October 1, 2002, www.hudson.org/index.cfm?fuseaction=publication_details&id=1979. Reproduced by permission.

used—such as animal manure or nitrogen-fixing legume plants, such as beans or clover, called "green manures." But all of this biological nitrogen requires land to produce it. As a consequence, a typical self-reliant organic farm has one-third or more of its land area devoted to producing organic nitrogen for growing the next crop.

---

*More efficient food production, not organic farming, is the only alternative to mass human starvation or widespread destruction of wildlands for agriculture.*

---

Hence, extending this organic ethic globally would gobble up vast amounts of land area for organic fertilizer production. Farmers of "non-organic" produce, by contrast, often use "synthetic" nitrogen that has been extracted from the atmosphere, which is 78 percent nitrogen. Essentially, no land is required to produce it. The industrial process can be fueled by any energy source available, including renewables such as solar or wind, and it is entirely sustainable.

The ultimate irony is that plants can only utilize nitrogen in the *in*organic form—the form delivered by "synthetic" fertilizers. One of the reasons for the lower crop yields of organic farms is the too-slow mineralization of nitrogen from organic materials in the soil, which leads to nutrient deficiencies.

How much land would an all-organic world eat up? Dr. Vaclav Smil, author of *Enriching the Earth*, estimates that it would require an additional 8 billion cattle to produce enough manure to replace the synthetic nitrogen currently used in the world. That's over and above the 1.2 billion cattle already on the planet. Where would we pasture them all?

## Land Cannot All Be Fertilized Organically

In the United States, farmers use about 11 million tons of synthetic nitrogen each year. To replace that with animal manure would require an additional 1 billion cattle. Considering that it takes 2 to 30 acres of pasture to support each animal, we're talking about 2 to 30 billion acres of land compared with the 2.1 billion acres that comprise the entire continental United States. We simply don't have nearly enough land to make the switch over to organic farming.

Instead of animal manure, we could grow green manure crops, but the land requirements would still be huge and unsustainable. Denmark proved this with a government-commissioned study of what converting the country to 100 percent organic would involve. (The Danes are a very politically correct bunch.) The Bichel committee's report, published in 1999, concluded that converting to organic would mean a whopping 47 percent decrease in food production.

The main reason for the productivity decline was not the lower yields in organic fields (although the yields are indeed lower), but rather the need to devote so much land to organic nitrogen production. The report was no industry hack-job, either: the former president of the Danish Society for the Conservation of Nature led the committee.

## Organic Foods Cannot Feed the World

This is an issue that must be resolved now. The world's human population is expected to increase another 50 percent during the next half-century, reaching a peak of roughly 9 billion. Moreover, most of these new mouths will probably have high enough incomes to afford high-quality diets. Combined, these two forces are expected to increase global food demand by 250 to 300 percent over the next fifty years. According to the United Nations Food and Agriculture Organization, humanity is already farming more than one-third of the planet's entire land area. More efficient food production, not organic farming, is the only alternative to mass human starvation or widespread destruction of wildlands for agriculture.

The *Newsweek* article ended with the statement that "an organic ethic could be the very key to our survival." But organic agriculture just wastes too much land for this to be true. If we are to have any hope of conserving the world's remaining biodiversity and wildlife habitat while feeding everyone, organic foods must remain the choice of a few lucky rich people in the world's most prosperous countries.

# Organic Farming Can Lead to Soil Depletion and Widespread Starvation

*Ronald Bailey*

*Ronald Bailey is science correspondent for* Reason, *a libertarian magazine. He is the author of* Liberation Biology: The Moral and Scientific Case for the Biotech Revolution *(Prometheus, 2005).*

Organic food production is growing by leaps and bounds in the United States. Many consumers are willing to pay premium prices for organic fruits, vegetables, and meats, convinced that they are helping the earth and eating healthier.

Swiss scientists at the Research Institute for Organic Agriculture have just published a twenty-one-year study in *Science* comparing two types of organic farming with two types of conventional agriculture. The results initially seem to back up those consumer beliefs, and the press has described the research as showing that organic farms are "viable" (to quote the *Los Angeles Times*) and "more efficient" (to quote Reuters). But don't rush out just yet to Whole Foods to stock up on organic arugula or chard.

Organic farming boils down to essentially two principles: Soluble mineral inputs, such as artificial nitrogen fertilizer, are forbidden, and so is the use of synthetic herbicides and pesticides. Another of the organic systems tested by the Swiss scientists, called bio-dynamic, was dreamed up by the German "anthroposophist" mystic Rudolf Steiner in the 1920s. Biodynamic farming uses such novel preparations as manure fermented in a cow's horn that is buried in the soil for six months

Ronald Bailey, "Organic Alchemy: Organic Farming Could Kill Billions of People," *Reason Online*, June 5, 2002. Copyright 2002 by Reason Foundation, 3415 S. Sepulveda Blvd., Suite 400, Los Angeles, CA 90034, www.reason.com. Reproduced by permission.

through autumn and winter. To these original principles, organic farmers' organizations have recently proscribed growing genetically enhanced crops.

## Organic Farming Is Less Productive

One of the most frequent criticisms of organic agriculture is that it is not as productive as conventional farming. The Swiss scientists confirmed this: Their organic plots were on average 20 percent less productive than conventional plots. For potatoes, organic production was about 40 percent lower. The researchers also point out that "cereal crop yields in Europe typically are 60 to 70 percent of those under conventional management." Furthermore, they dispelled the notion that organic crops are superior food by noting, "There were minor differences between the farming systems in food quality."

---

*Is organic agriculture sustainable over the long run? Again, the fine print says no. . . . Organic farming is mining the soil of its vital minerals.*

---

The Swiss scientists based their claims for greater organic "efficiency" chiefly on the differences in the amount of energy used to produce the crops. Since the same horticultural techniques were used on both conventional and organic plots, the difference in energy use was mostly the result of counting the energy used to produce inorganic fertilizers and pesticides. On this basis, the researchers claim in their *Science* article that organic farms use about 50 percent less energy. However, looking at the fine print, one discovers that "since crop yields were considerably higher in the conventional systems, the difference in energy needed to produce a crop unit was only 19 percent lower in the organic systems."

## Organic Farming Is Not Sustainable

Secondly, the researchers declare that they found nutrients "in the organic systems to be 34 to 51 percent lower than in conventional systems, whereas mean crop yield was only 20 percent lower over a period of 21 years." But—to ask the organic advocates' own question—is organic agriculture sustainable over the long run? Again, the fine print says no. As their research confirms, organic farming is mining the soil of its vital minerals, particularly phosphorus and potassium. Eventually, as these minerals are used up, organic crop production will fall below its already low level. Conventional farming, on the other hand, restores mineral balances through fertilization. "The Swiss researchers are not thinking globally, they're only acting locally," says Alex Avery, director of research for the Hudson Institute's Center for Global Food Issues. Avery points out that organic farming can supply food for niche markets of affluent consumers but cannot feed a hungry world. Other methods of food production can. In his new book *Enriching the Earth* [2001], the University of Manitoba agronomist Vaclav Smil credits the Haber-Bosch method of producing nitrogen fertilizer, invented in 1909, with sustaining two billion people today.

Synthetic fertilizers now supply 40 percent of all the nitrogen used by crop plants. Without this artificially produced fertilizer, farmers would simply not be able to grow the crops necessary to feed the world's population. Organic sources of nitrogen, such as animal manure and leguminous plants, would supply only about a quarter of the nitrogen needed. (The remainder comes from rain and lightning.) Other inventions, such as high-yielding crop varieties and modern farm equipment, have also been vital to boosting food supplies. For example, when farm tractors arrived after the 1920s, they replaced draft animals that consumed a quarter of the crops grown in the United States.

Keep in mind that plants cannot tell the difference between "natural" sources of nitrogen, phosphorus, and potassium and "artificial" sources of those elements. The reason is that there *is* no difference, outside the minds of organic farmers.

---

*The greatest catastrophe that the human race could face this century is not global warming but a global conversion to "organic farming."*

---

## Enhanced Conventional Methods Are Superior to Organic Ones

The Swiss researchers did find some true benefits from organic farming, including greater water retention by the soil and a higher presence of beneficial insects. Unfortunately, they did not test their organic systems against the newest form of conventional agriculture, no-till farming combined with genetically enhanced crops. This uses much less energy and less pesticides than the old-fashioned systems examined by the Swiss scientists.

Since no-till farmers don't plow, their tractors use less fuel. Also, since weed control is achieved using environmentally benign herbicides instead of mechanical removal through plowing, even more fuel is saved. Finally, no-till farmers use less insecticide, since genetically enhanced crops can protect themselves against pests. Against all this, organic farming's 19 percent energy advantage would likely disappear.

No-till farming matches several other advantages of organic agriculture as well. Both methods offer improved soil structure, more water retention, greatly reduced soil erosion, less pesticide and fertilizer runoff, and a higher presence of beneficial insects. Although organic farmers refuse to see it, switching to genetically enhanced crops would go a long way toward accomplishing their avowed goals of restoring their land and helping the natural environment.

## Organic Farming Offers No Long Term Public Good

One final argument often offered by organic enthusiasts is that organic farming is more profitable. Of course, the reason organic foods command a premium at supermarkets is that so many consumers have been bamboozled into thinking that they are somehow superior. If organic farming became widespread, that premium would dissipate and take its higher profitability with it.

As the Cambridge chemist John Emsley recently concluded, "The greatest catastrophe that the human race could face this century is not global warming but a global conversion to 'organic farming'—an estimated 2 billion people would perish." News reports may hail the Swiss study as proving that organic farming is sustainable, but it actually did the opposite.

# The Organic Movement Will Not Enact Real Environmental Changes

*The Economist*

*The* Economist *is a British newsweekly focusing on international politics and business news.*

If you think you can make the planet better by clever shopping, think again. You might make it worse

"You don't have to wait for government to move ... the really fantastic thing about Fairtrade is that you can go shopping!" So said a representative of the Fairtrade movement in a British newspaper this year. Similarly Marion Nestle, a nutritionist at New York University, argues that "when you choose organics, you are voting for a planet with fewer pesticides, richer soil and cleaner water supplies."

## Organic Food: Is It Politics or Just Shopping?

The idea that shopping is the new politics is certainly seductive. Never mind the ballot box: vote with your supermarket trolley [cart] instead. Elections occur relatively rarely, but you probably go shopping several times a month, providing yourself with lots of opportunities to express your opinions. If you are worried about the environment, you might buy organic food; if you want to help poor farmers, you can do your bit by buying Fairtrade products; or you can express a dislike of evil multinational companies and rampant globalisation by buying only local produce. And the best bit is that shopping, unlike voting, is fun; so you can do good and enjoy yourself at the same time.

Sadly, it's not that easy. There are good reasons to doubt the claims made about three of the most popular varieties of "ethical" food: organic food, Fairtrade food, and local food. People who want to make the world a better place cannot do so by shifting their shopping habits: transforming the planet requires duller disciplines, like politics.

---

*Moving food around in big, carefully packed lorries [trucks], as supermarkets do, may in fact be the most efficient way to transport the stuff.*

---

## Buy Organic, Destroy the Rain Forest

Organic food, which is grown without man-made pesticides and fertilisers, is generally assumed to be more environmentally friendly than conventional intensive farming, which is heavily reliant on chemical inputs. But it all depends what you mean by "environmentally friendly". Farming is inherently bad for the environment: Since humans took it up around 11,000 years ago, the result has been deforestation on a massive scale. But following the "green revolution" [an effort to increase the food-producing capacity of developing countries through improved strains of grain, fertilization, and irrigation] of the 1960s greater use of chemical fertiliser has tripled grain yields with very little increase in the area of land under cultivation. Organic methods, which rely on crop rotation, manure and compost in place of fertiliser, are far less intensive. So producing the world's current agricultural output organically would require several times as much land as is currently cultivated. There wouldn't be much room left for the rainforest.

Fairtrade food is designed to raise poor farmers' incomes. It is sold at a higher price than ordinary food, with a subsidy passed back to the farmer. But prices of agricultural commodities are low because of overproduction. By propping up the price, the Fairtrade system encourages farmers to produce more of these commodities rather than diversifying into other crops and so depresses prices—thus achieving, for most farmers, exactly the opposite of what the initiative is intended to do. And since only a small fraction of the mark-up on Fairtrade foods actually goes to the farmer—most goes to the retailer—the system gives rich consumers an inflated impression of their largesse and makes alleviating poverty seem too easy.

## The Fallacy of Local Food

Surely the case for local food, produced as close as possible to the consumer in order to minimise "food miles" and, by extension, carbon emissions, is clear? Surprisingly, it is not. A study of Britain's food system found that nearly half of food-vehicle miles, (miles travelled by vehicles carrying food) were driven by cars going to and from the shops. Most people live closer to a supermarket than a farmer's market, so more local food could mean more food-vehicle miles. Moving food around in big, carefully packed lorries [trucks], as supermarkets do, may in fact be the most efficient way to transport the stuff.

*There is an enormous appetite for change and widespread frustration that governments are not doing enough to preserve the environment . . .*

What's more, once the energy used in production as well as transport is taken into account, local food may turn out to be even less green. Producing lamb in New Zealand and shipping it to Britain uses less energy than producing British lamb, because farming in New Zealand is less energy-intensive. And the local-food movement's aims, of course, contradict those of the Fairtrade movement, by discouraging rich-country consumers from buying poor-country produce. But since the local-food movement looks suspiciously like old-fashioned protectionism masquerading as concern for the environment, helping poor countries is presumably not the point.

## Appetite for Change Calls for Structural Changes

The aims of much of the ethical-food movement—to protect the environment, to encourage development, and to redress the distortions in global trade—are admirable. The problems lie in the means, not the ends. No amount of Fairtrade coffee will eliminate poverty, and all the organic asparagus in the world will not save the planet. Some of the stuff sold under an ethical label may even leave the world in a worse state and its poor farmers poorer than they otherwise would be.

So what should the ethically minded consumer do? Things that are less fun than shopping, alas. Real change will require action by governments, in the form of a global carbon tax; reform of the world trade system; and the abolition of agricultural tariffs and subsidies, notably Europe's monstrous common agricultural policy, which coddles rich farmers and prices those in the poor world out of the European market. Proper free trade would be by far the best way to help poor farmers. Taxing carbon would price the cost of emissions into the price of goods, and retailers would then have an incentive to source locally if it saved energy. But these changes will come about only through difficult, international, political deals that the world's governments have so far failed to do.

The best thing about the spread of the ethical-food movement is that it offers grounds for hope. It sends a signal that there is an enormous appetite for change and widespread frustration that governments are not doing enough to preserve the environment, reform world trade or encourage development. Which suggests that, if politicians put these options on the political menu, people might support them. The idea of changing the world by voting with your trolley may be beguiling. But if consumers really want to make a difference, it is at the ballot box that they need to vote.

# Affordable Organic Food Is Not Sustainable

## James Joyner

*James Joyner is the founder of the political blog* Outside the Beltway *and a regular contributor to the online technology/ politics Web site* TCS Daily. *In the following viewpoint he comments on the June 4, 2006, edition of the* New York Times Magazine.

There's an interestig piece in today's NYT Magazine noting that by attempting to make organic food—now derided by many as an elitist luxury—cheap enough for the masses to afford, Wal-Mart may be undermining the very things that make organics desirable in the first place.

Assuming that it's possible at all, how exactly would Wal-Mart get the price of organic food down to a level just 10 percent higher than that of its everyday food? To do so would virtually guarantee that Wal-Mart's version of cheap organic food is not sustainable, at least not in any meaningful sense of that word. To index the price of organic to the price of conventional is to give up, right from the start, on the idea, once enshrined in the organic movement, that food should be priced not high or low but responsibly. As the organic movement has long maintained, cheap industrial food is cheap only because the real costs of producing it are not reflected in the price at the checkout. Rather, those costs are charged to the environment, in the form of soil depletion and pollution (industrial agriculture is now our biggest polluter); to the public purse, in the form of subsidies to conventional commodity farmers; to the public health, in the form of an epidemic of diabetes and obesity that is ex-

James Joyner, "Wal-Mart Ruining Organics for the Elites?" *Outside the Beltway*, June 4, 2006, www.outsidethebeltway.com/archives/2006/wal-mart_ruining_organics_for_the _elites/. Reproduced by permission.

pected to cost the economy more than $100 billion per year; and to the welfare of the farm- and food-factory workers, not to mention the well-being of the animals we eat. As Wendell Berry once wrote, the motto of our conventional food system—at the center of which stands Wal-Mart, the biggest purveyor of cheap food in America—should be: Cheap at any price!

## Can Cheap Organic Be Real Organic?

To say you can sell organic food for 10 percent more than you sell irresponsibly priced food suggests that you don't really get it—that you plan to bring business-as-usual principles of industrial "efficiency" and "economies of scale" to a system of food production that was supposed to mimic the logic of natural systems rather than that of the factory.

---

*The industrialization of organic agriculture, which Wal-Mart's involvement will only deepen, has already given us "organic feedlots"—two words that I never thought would find their way into the same clause.*

---

Remember, now, at the moment most people simply cannot afford "organic" food. They're consuming food that's been sprayed with pesticides and prepared with preservatives to give it a long shelf life. And whatever cost to the environment that comes from these practices is already being borne. So, we're comparing an ideal—growing foods that yield some health gains to the consumer in addition to various environmental benefits—that does not presently exist at anything but a niche level because of cost against a proposed reality where the health gains are made possible for the masses but without the ancillary environmental gain.

We have already seen what happens when the logic of the factory is applied to organic food production. The industrialization of organic agriculture, which Wal-Mart's involvement will only deepen, has already given us "organic feed-lots"—two words that I never thought would find their way into the same clause. To supply the escalating demand for cheap organic milk, agribusiness [the system of large-scale agriculture and food production] companies are setting up 5,000-head dairies, often in the desert. These milking cows never touch a blade of grass, instead spending their days standing around a dry-lot "loafing area" munching organic grain—grain that takes a toll on both the animals' health (these ruminants evolved to eat grass, after all) and the nutritional value of their milk. But this is the sort of milk (deficient in beta-carotene and the "good fats"—like omega 3s and CLA—that come from grazing cows on grass) we're going to see a lot more of in the supermarket as long as Wal-Mart determines to keep organic milk cheap.

But isn't that how affordable milk is produced now? Why don't we compare Wal-Martized organic milk to the status-quo?

## Cheap Organic Will Become Imported Organic

We're also going to see more organic milk—and organic foods of all kinds—coming from places like New Zealand. The globalization of organic food is already well under way: at Whole Foods you can buy organic asparagus flown in from Argentina, raspberries from Mexico, grass-fed meat from New Zealand. In an era of energy scarcity, the purchase of such products does little to advance the ideal of sustainability that once upon a time animated the organic movement. These foods may contain no pesticides, but they are drenched in petroleum even so.

No, they're not. They're merely transported. But don't we transport goods globally now in consuming non-organic foods?

# Organic Will Move from Diversified to Concentrated

Whether produced domestically or not, organic meat will increasingly come not from mixed, polyculture farms growing a variety of species (a practice that makes it possible to recycle nutrients between plants and animals) but from ever-bigger Confined Animal Feeding Operations, or CAFOs which, apart from using organic feed and abjuring antibiotics, are little different from their conventional counterparts. Yes, the federal organic rules say the animals should have "access to the outdoors," but in practice this often means providing them with a tiny exercise yard or, in the case of one organic egg producer in New England, a screened-in concrete "porch"—a view of the outdoors. Herein lies one of the deeper paradoxes of practicing organic agriculture on an industrial scale: big, single-species CAFOs are even more precarious than their conventional cousins, since they can't use antibiotics to keep the thousands of animals living in close confinement indoors from becoming sick. So organic CAFO-hands (to call them farmhands seems overly generous) keep the free ranging to a minimum and then keep their fingers crossed.

Okay. But how would mass-produced organic meat compare to mass-produced non-organic meat? And, would the niche organic products now available still be available for those willing and able to invest in ensuring that the animals grown to be killed and eaten have enjoyable lives? If so, what's the harm?

Wal-Mart will buy its organic food from whichever producers can produce it most cheaply, and these will not be the sort of farmers you picture when you hear the word "organic." Big supermarkets want to do business only with big farmers growing lots of the same thing, not because big monoculture farms are any more efficient (they aren't) but because it's easier to buy all your carrots from a single megafarm than to contract with hundreds of smaller growers.

The "transaction costs" are lower, even when the price and the quality are the same. This is just one of the many ways in which the logic of industrial capitalism and the logic of biology on a farm come into conflict. At least in the short run, the logic of capitalism usually prevails.

So? What has that to do with healthy food or a healthy environment? Is organic food about a social ideal or about science?

## Can Organic Survive Mainstreaming?

Wal-Mart's push into the organic market won't do much for small organic farmers, that seems plain enough. But it may also spell trouble for the big growers it will favor. Wal-Mart has a reputation for driving down prices by squeezing its suppliers, especially after those suppliers have invested heavily to boost production to feed the Wal-Mart maw. Having done that, the supplier will find itself at Wal-Mart's mercy when the company decides it no longer wants to pay a price that enables the farmer to make a living. When that happens, the notion of responsibly priced food will be sacrificed to the imperatives of survival, and the pressure to cut corners will become irresistible.

As opposed to the status quo, where farmers charge whatever they want, make fabulous incomes, and cut no corners?

I understand the utopian ideals that many advocates of organic foods are pushing and think many of them are worthwhile. They are not, unfortunately, economically sustainable. I shop at Whole Foods several times a week and pay substantially more for groceries than I used to at Safeway and other supermarkets. I don't do it because of a political agenda but because I think the food, especially the meats, taste better. Fortunately, I live in an area where such options are available to me and where incomes are high enough that I can afford it.

The reality, though, is that most people simply cannot afford to pay $3 for a dozen eggs, $6 a pound for chicken, or

$15–30 a pound for steak on a regular basis. It's literally more expensive to buy groceries at Whole Foods and prepare your own meals than to go out to dinner at a chain restaurant like Applebee's or Ruby Tuesdays. I couldn't have done that on an assistant professor's salary in south Alabama even if there was such a store available. Certainly, people working for hourly wages in the service economy couldn't.

The perfect should not be allowed to become the enemy of the good. In an ideal world, local farmers would produce delicious foods grown without any harm to the environment at prices we could all afford while simultaneously making an excellent living. The livestock would all live happy lives, singing their little animal songs, dying a natural death and yet remaining tender and tasty. We would then get together and cook them over our campfires which produce no smoke, sing our little camp songs, and eat our meals in perfect harmony.

That world, unfortunately, does not exist.

# Organizations to Contact

*The editors have compiled the following list of organizations concerned with the issues debated in this book. The descriptions are derived from materials provided by the organizations. All have publications or information available for interested readers. The list was compiled on the date of publication of the present volume; names, addresses, phone and fax numbers, and e-mail and Web site addresses may change. Be aware that many organizations take several weeks or longer to respond to inquiries, so allow as much time as possible.*

**Action Against Hunger USA (AAH)**
247 West Thirty-Seventh St., Suite 1201
New York, NY   10018
(212) 967-7800 • fax: (212) 967-5480
e-mail: info@actionagainsthunger.org
Web site: www.actionagainsthunger.org

Action Against Hunger USA is a wing of Action Against Hunger, an international nongovernmental organization that is a leader in the fight against hunger. The organization provides emergency relief and treatments for malnutrition. AAH publishes the newsletter *Response.*

**American Council on Science and Health (ACSH)**
1995 Broadway, Second Floor, New York, NY   10023-5860
(212) 362-7044 • fax: (212) 362-4919
e-mail: acsh@acsh.org
Web site: www.acsh.org

ACSH is a consumer education organization that is concerned with issues relating to food and nutrition. It provides consumers with scientific evaluations of food and information on health hazards and benefits. Articles on food safety and publications such as *Irradiated Foods* and *The Role of Beef in the American Diet* are available on the Web site.

## American Dietetic Association

120 South Riverside Plaza, Suite 2000
Chicago, IL 60606-6995
(800) 877-1600
Web site: www.eatright.org

The American Dietetic Association is the largest organization of food and nutrition professionals in the United States. It works to shape the food choices of the public for optimal nutrition and health. The association publishes newsletters for members, as well as the monthly *Journal of the American Dietetic Association* and booklets, fact sheets, and pamphlets about nutrition.

## American Obesity Association (AOA)

1250 Twenty-Fourth St. NW, Suite 300
Washington, DC 20037
(202) 776-7711 • fax: (202) 776-7712
e-mail: executive@obesity.org
www.obesity.org leads to "The Obesity Society."

The goal of the AOA is to teach society that obesity is a disease and to develop strategies to deal with the epidemic. Its activities include education about and research on obesity. Fact sheets on obesity are available on the Web site.

## Animal Agricultural Alliance

PO Box 9522, Arlington, Virginia 22209
(703) 562-5160
e-mail: info@animalagalliance.org
Web site: www.animalagalliance.org

The alliance consists of individuals, organizations, and companies who want to provide consumers with accurate information about the importance of animal agriculture in efforts to feed the world. It provides information on agroterrorism and factory farms. Alliance members have access to newsletters.

## Center for Consumer Freedom
PO Box 27414, Washington, DC   20038
(202) 463-7112
Web site: www.consumerfreedom.com

The Center for Consumer Freedom is a nonprofit coalition of restaurants, food companies, and consumers that aims to promote personal responsibility and protect consumer choices. Opinion pieces on food safety and obesity, cartoons, and daily news archive can be found on the center's Web site.

## Food and Agriculture Organization of the United Nations (FAO)
Viale delle Terme di Caracalla, Rome   00100
   Italy
(+39) 06 57051 • fax: (+39) 06 570 53152
e-mail: FAO-HQ@fao.org
Web site: www.fao.org

FAO is an organization that leads the global effort to fight hunger. It provides information on hunger and provides a neutral forum for all countries to debate hunger policy and negotiate agreements. FAO also helps developing nations improve their agriculture practices. Publications available for purchase from the Web site include *Human Nutrition in the Developing World* and the annual *State of Food and Agriculture.*

## Food First/Institute for Food Development and Policy
398 Sixtieth St., Oakland, CA   94618
(510) 654-4400 • fax: (510) 654-4551
Web site: www.foodfirst.org

The goal of Food First/Institute for Food Development and Policy is to eliminate the injustices that cause hunger. The institute believes that hunger persists because hungry people lack the resources to produce or buy food. It supports land reform and sustainable agricultural practices. Its publications include *Food First Backgrounders, News and Views,* books, and fact sheets.

**National Institutes of Health (NIH)**
9000 Rockville Pike, Bethesda, MD   20892
(301) 496-4000
e-mail: NIHinfo@od.nih.gov
Web site: www.nih.gov

The goal of the NIH is to discover new information that will improve everyone's health. It supports and conducts research and helps spread medical information. The NIH publishes brochures, online fact sheets, and handbooks with information about obesity.

**Organic Consumers Association (OCA)**
6771 South Silver Hill Drive, Finland, MN   55603
(218) 226-4164 • (218) 353-7652
Web site: www.organicconsumers.org

OCA is a nonprofit organization that focuses exclusively on the interests of America's estimated 10 million organic consumers. The organization deals with issues such as food safety, genetic engineering, and industrial agriculture. The Web site provides links to news and articles on issues such as irradiation, organic food, and genetically engineered food. The association also publishes the newsletters *Organic Bytes* and *Organic View*.

**Organic Farming Research Foundation**
PO Box 440, Santa Cruz, CA   95061
(831) 426-6606 • fax: (831) 426-6670
Web site: www.ofrf.org/

The foundation is a nonprofit organization that sponsors research on organic farming and disseminates the results to farmers, the public, and policy makers. It publishes the newsletter *Information Bulletin*.

**Oxfam America**
226 Causeway St., 5th Floor, Boston, MA   02114
(800) 77-OXFAM • fax: (617) 728-2594

e-mail: info@oxfamamerica.org
Web site: www.oxfamamerica.org

Oxfam America is an affiliate of Oxfam International, which is a group of twelve organizations that are working in more than one hundred nations to find solutions to poverty and related issues, such as hunger and famine. Oxfam has worked in disasters and emergency situations for over sixty years. The organization publishes papers relating to hunger and famine, such as *HIV/AIDS and Food Insecurity in Southern Africa* and *Food Aid or Hidden Dumping? Separating Wheat from Chaff.*

### U.S. Department of Agriculture (USDA)
1400 Independence Ave. SW, Washington, DC   20250
Web site: www.usda.gov

The USDA's primary purpose is to work with farmers and ranchers. In addition, it also oversees federal antihunger efforts such as the food stamp and school lunch programs. The USDA is also responsible for the safety of meat, eggs, and poultry. Publications available on the Web site include *Food & Nutrition Research Briefs* and *Agricultural Research* magazine.

### U.S. Food and Drug Administration Center for Food Safety and Applied Nutrition (CFSAN)
5100 Paint Branch Pkwy., College Park, MD   20740-3835
Web site: vm.cfsan.fda.gov/list.html

The mission of CFSAN is to protect the public's health by guaranteeing that the U.S. food supply is safe, sanitary, and correctly labeled. The center is part of the Food and Drug Administration (FDA), a regulatory agency that is responsible for consumer safety. Papers and congressional testimony relating to food safety are available on the Web site, along with consumer advice.

# Bibliography

## Books

Paul Campos

*The Obesity Myth: Why America's Obsession with Weight Is Hazardous.* New York: Gotham Books, 2004.

Christopher D Cook

*Diet for a Dead Planet: How the Food Industry Is Killing Us.* New York: New Press, 2004.

Ann Cooper

*Bitter Harvest: A Chef's Perspective on the Hidden Dangers in the Foods We Eat and What You Can Do About It.* New York: Routledge, 2000.

Caroline Smith DeWaal, et al.

*Outbreak Alert! Closing the Gaps in Our Federal Food-Safety Net.* Washington, DC: Center for Science in the Public Interest, 2005.

Steve Ettlinger

*Twinkie, Deconstructed: My Journey to Discover How the Ingredients Found in Processed Foods are Grown, Mined (Yes, Mined), and Manipulated into What America Eats.* New York: Hudson Street, 2007.

Food and Agriculture Organization of the United Nations

*The State of Food and Agriculture, 2003–2004.* Rome: Food and Agriculture Organization, 2004.

Susanne Freidberg *French Beans and Food Scares: Culture and Commerce in an Anxious Age.* New York: Oxford University Press, 2004.

Walter Gratzer *Terrors of the Table: The Curious History of Nutrition.* Oxford, UK: Oxford University Press, 2005.

Brian Halweil *Eat Here: Homegrown Pleasures in a Global Supermarket.* New York: Norton, 2004.

Kathleen Hart *Eating in the Dark: America's Experiment with Genetically Engineered Food.* New York: Pantheon, 2002.

Carolyn Johnsen *Raising a Stink: The Struggle over Factory Hog Farms in Nebraska.* Lincoln: University of Nebraska Press, 2003.

Barbara Kingsolver with Steven L. Hopp and Camille Kingsolver *Animal, Vegetable, Miracle: A Year of Food Life.* New York: HarperCollins, 2007.

Frances Moore Lappé and Anna Lappé *Hope's Edge: The Next Diet for a Small Planet.* New York: Tarcher, 2003.

Susan Linn *Consuming Kids.* New York: New Press, 2004.

Paisan Loaharanu *Irradiated Foods*, 5⁰ ed. New York: American Council on Science and Health, 2005.

George McGovern, Bob Dole, and Donald E. Messer — *Ending Hunger Now: A Challenge to Persons of Faith*. Minneapolis: Fortress, 2005.

Henry I. Miller and Gregory Conko — *The Frankenfood Myth: How Protest and Politics Threaten the Biotech Revolution*. New York: Praeger, 2004.

Erik Millstone and Tim Lang — *The Penguin Atlas of Food: Who Eats What, Where, and Why*. New York: Penguin, 2003.

Marion Nestle — *Food Politics: How the Food Industry Influences Nutrition and Health*. Berkeley: University of California Press, 2002.

Marion Nestle — *What to Eat: An Aisle-by-Aisle Guide to Savvy Food Choices and Good Eating*. Berkeley: University of California Press, 2006.

Danielle Nierenberg — *Happier Meals: Rethinking the Global Meat Industry*. Washington, DC: Worldwatch Institute, 2005.

Michael Pollan — *The Omnivore's Dilemma: A Natural History of Four Meals*. New York: Penguin, 2006.

Rich Pirog, et al. — *Food, Fuel, and Freeways*. Ames: University of Iowa, Leopold Center for Sustainable Agriculture, 2001.

Joel Salatin — *Holy Cows and Hog Heaven: The Food Buyer's Guide to Farm Friendly Food*. Swoope, VA: Polyface, 2004.

Eric Schlosser          *Fast Food Nation: The Dark Side of the All-American Meal.* New York: Perennial, 2002.

Lee Silver             *Challenging Nature: The Clash of Science and Spirituality at the New Frontiers of Life.* New York: Ecco, 2006.

Donald D. Stull        *Slaughterhouse Blues: The Meat and Poultry Industry in North America.* Belmont, CA: Thomson/Wadsworth, 2004.
and Michael J. Broadway

## Periodicals

Alex A. Avery          "Organic Hypocrisy," *American Council on Science and Health*, September 19, 2003.

Dennis Avery and       "No More Chicken Run," *Wall Street Journal* [European edition], August 26, 2005.
Alex A. Avery

Burkhard Bilger        "The Lunchroom Rebellion," *New Yorker*, September 4, 2006.

Aaron L. Brody         "What's Fresh About Fresh-Cut," *Food Technology*, January 2005.

Jane Brody             "Beware Food Companies' Health Claims," *New York Times*, September 21, 2004.

Marian Burros          "The Food Pyramid Takes Its Show on the Road," *New York Times*, January 17, 2007.

Marian Burros — "Government Offers Guidelines to Fresh-Food Industry," *New York Times*, March 13, 2007.

David B. Caruso — "Deal Reached on Improving School Snacks," *Minneapolis Star Tribune*, October 7, 2006.

Center for Consumer Freedom — "*E. coli* Is 'All Natural' Too," November 9, 2006.

Ian Duncan — "Welfare Problems of Poultry," in John Benson and Bernard Rollin, eds. *The Well-Being of Farm Animals.* Ames: Iowa State Press, 2004.

Sarah Ellison — "Despite Big Health Concerns, Food Industry Can't Shake Salt," *Wall Street Journal*, February 25, 2005.

Michael Fumento — "Obesity Goes to the Dogs," *American Spectator*, January 18, 2007.

Jon Gertner — "The Virtue in $6 Heirloom Tomatoes," *New York Times Magazine*, June 6, 2004.

Denise Grady — "When Bad Things Come From 'Good' Food," *New York Times*, January 2, 2007.

Nathaniel Johnson — "Swine of the Times: The Making of the Modern Pig," *Harper's*, May 2006.

David Karp — "For Raspberries, Ubiquity (at a Price)," *New York Times*, July 7, 2004.

Paisan Loaharanu    "Info on Irradiated Food for School Lunch Misleads," *American Council on Science and Health*, October 3, 2003.

Seth Lubove    "Food Porn," *Forbes*, February 14, 2005.

Juliane Malveaux    "Got Milk? Got Hormones?—Exploiting Food Fear," *Huffington Post*, January 2, 2007.

Andrew Martin    "Makers of Sodas Try a New Pitch: They're Healthy," *New York Times*, March 6, 2007.

Andrew Martin    "Organic Milk Debate," *Chicago Tribune*, January 10, 2005.

Daniel McGinn    "The Green Machine," *Newsweek*, March 21, 2005.

Matt McKinney    "Organic Milk: It's not a Black-and-White Issue," *Minneapolis Star Tribune*, August 12, 2006.

Henry I. Miller and Gregory Conko    "The Origins of 'Biotechnology,'" *CEI's Monthly Planet*, October 2004.

Steven Milloy    "Food Police Indict SpongeBob," *FoxNews.com*, January 19, 2006.

*Minneapolis Star Tribune*    "Biotech Foods: A Cat That Won't Stay Bagged," [editorial] August 27, 2006.

*New York Times*    "The Food Pyramid Scheme," [editorial] September 1, 2004.

Marina Palomba      "The Truth About Advertising Food to Children," *IPA News*, August 14, 2003.

Andrew Pollack      "Maker Warns of Scarcity of Hormone for Dairy Cows," *New York Times*, January 27, 2004.

Michael Pollan      "Our National Eating Disorder," *New York Times Magazine*, October 17, 2004.

Barry M. Popkin     "Pour Better or Pour Worse? How Beverages Stack Up," *Nutrition Action Healthletter*, June 2006.

Roy Rivenburg       "Scaling Food Pyramid Makes One Guinea Pig a Lesser Man," *Los Angeles Times*, February 19, 2005.

David Schardt       "Milking the Data: Does Dairy Burn More Fat? Don't Bet Your Bottom on It," *Nutrition Action Healthletter*, September 2005.

Melanie Warner      "Lines Drawn for Big Suit over Sodas," *New York Times*, December 7, 2005.

Melanie Warner      "Striking Back at the Food Police," *New York Times*, June 12, 2005.

George F. Will      "What We Owe What We Eat," *Newsweek*, July 18, 2005.

Nicholas Zamiska    "How Milk Got a Major Boost from Food Panel," *Wall Street Journal*, October 12, 2005.

# Index